Pathways
from
Quilt
Top to
Quilted

Sally Terry

American Quilter's Society
P. O. Box 3290 • Paducah, KY 42002-3290
www.AmericanQuilter.com

Located in Paducah, Kentucky, the American Quilter's Society (AQS) is dedicated to promoting the accomplishments of today's quilters. Through its publications and events, AQS strives to honor today's quiltmakers and their work and to inspire future creativity and innovation in quiltmaking.

Executive Book Editor: Andi Milam Reynolds
Senior Book Editor: Linda Baxter Lasco
Copy Editor: Chrystal Abhalter
Graphic Design: Elaine Wilson
Cover Design: Michael Buckingham
Quilt Photography: Charles R. Lynch
How-To Photography: Sally Terry

Additional copies of this book may be ordered from the American Quilter's Society, PO Box 3290, Paducah, KY 42002-3290, or online at www.AmericanQuilter.com.

Text © 2011, Author, Sally Terry
Artwork © 2011, American Quilter's Society

Library of Congress Cataloging-in-Publication Data

Terry, Sally.
  Pathways from quilt top to quilted / by Sally Terry.
    p. cm.
  Includes bibliographical references.
  ISBN 978-1-57432-680-2
  1. Quilting--Technique. I. American Quilter's Society. II. Title.
  TT835.T3797 2011
  746.46--dc22
                    2010053311

Dedication

This book is dedicated to Sarah, my daughter and best friend, for her rock solid advice and beautiful outlook on life.

To my dedicated students, who have so much faith in me, you have taken the very same classes many many times over.

Tim, who always thinks I am better than I think I am and that I don't think big enough.

To Pam Heavrin, my longarm sister who inspired me to write *Hooked On Feathers* and so graciously allows me to borrow her thread. She is motivating and encouraging always.

TITLE PAGE: PRECIOUS PANSIES, detail. Full quilt on page 82.

LEFT: ZIGS ZAGS II, detail. Full quilt on page 74.

Introduction

From beginning to end, quilting is a delightful process. Just the hum of the needle is enough to send us into a heavenly state. All is right with the world.

While each tiny little step needs a decision that can make the task more complicated, most of us want a simple recipe to follow, and that is what this book is designed to give you—a path to follow from beginning to end. And I've thrown in a few twists, so you can make each creation truly your own with all the fanfare and none of the angst.

Hence, the title—*Pathways from Quilt Top to Quilted*. A simple step-by-step process for anything from a traditional sit-down machine to a large-format longarm quilting machine, this book will be your guide. In addition, I have provided a troubleshooting section right up front to help you along your way.

If you have not machine quilted before there is another book written earlier in my career that will teach you the moves—*Pathways to Better Quilting*, published by the American Quilter's Society. This will give you the all-important basics, from how to read a quilting pattern, where to focus your eyes, and how to move the machine or fabric in relation to the needle, to how to count and talk to yourself for consistent shapes and stitching. If you will forgive me, it has been called a "classic" by Midwest Book Review and a must for every quilter's bookshelf, from traditional sit-down machine to longarm.

Most of us do not start a quilting project with the intention of *not* finishing it. We love the ideas and the process involved and we have many projects in the works—at least one in every room of our home. With each new colorway, each new exciting fabric line or clever pattern, a new idea beckons to us.

Here are the easy steps and some new techniques to help you happily complete your projects. So, let the projects begin!

LEFT: **MORNING GARDEN**, detail. Made by Ulla Shierhorn, Paducah, KY, and quilted by the author. **POTPOURRI** pattern from the book *Simple Shapes Spectacular Quilts* by Kaffe Fassett and Liza Prior Lucy.

Contents

RIGHT: NATURE'S FIREWORKS, detail. Full quilt on page 16.

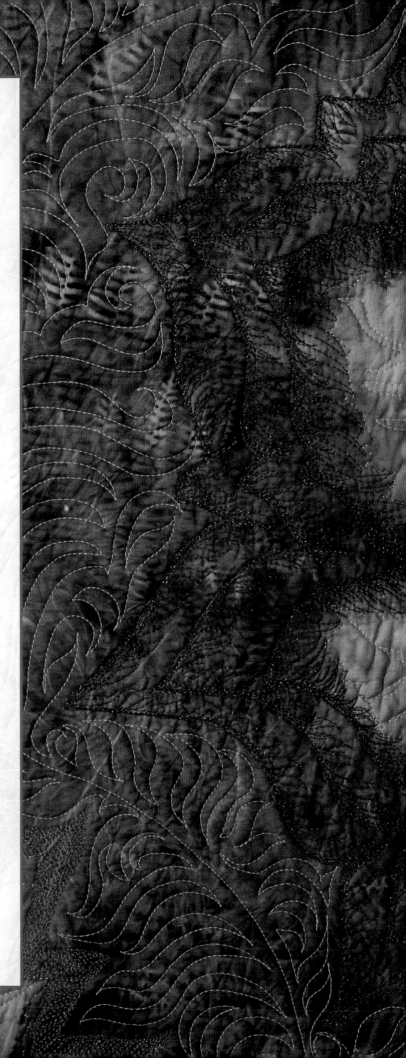

quilt page 00

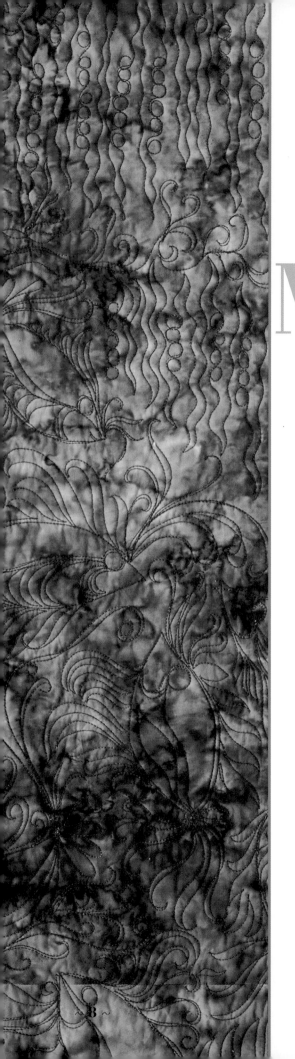

Avoid Trouble
from the Start

My goal is to make your quilting enjoyable and to provide fast and easy solutions for any problems you may encounter. I like addressing trouble spots first to get them out of the way. By knowing what the problems are we can avoid them altogether.

I have put these trouble spots in the order as you come to them in the quilting process. No one problem is more critical than the next.

UNSTABILIZED EDGES AND TOPS

Stay stitch ⅛" from the outer edge of the quilt top before loading it, especially if there are a lot of construction seams along the edges. Some of the stitching will be removed when the quilt is squared up and trimmed for the binding.

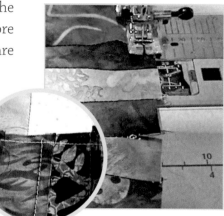

Use Fray Check® or other seam sealant on seams within the quilt that are not completely sewn. Apply from underneath or hand sew the loose seams closed. Quilting over these areas will help mask and secure them at the same time.

There are times when the entire quilt top needs to be stabilized with machine basting, especially if you will be using different threads

LEFT: SALT-WATER-BED AQUARIUM, detail of back. Full quilt on page 9.

and want to complete one thread color throughout the quilt top, then go back with the other colors. It also is appropriate for situations where the quilt sandwich will be removed from the frame before it is completed, to be reloaded later.

Larger quilt tops can be machine basted for hand or traditional machine quilting.

Check the batting package for the recommended distance between threadpaths. Use that distance to space the vertical and horizontal basting threads.

ABOVE: The first blocks I quilted were not stabilized and the quilting distorted the sashing. I stitched in the ditch around the rest of the blocks and you can see that it made a difference.

LEFT: SALT-WATER-BED AQUARIAM, 76" x 93". Made by Janet Coen, Golconda, IL, and quilted by the author.
AS TIME GOES BY pattern designed by Nicole Chambers-Kaya, Tiger Lily Press.

Use a basting stitch on quilts that need stabilizing when loaded on a track/frame and stitch in the following sequence:

1. Stitch all the verticals first, starting with the first vertical seam if it is less than the recommended threadpath distance from the edge of the quilt. If the distance is greater, then follow construction lines that are closer together.

2. Continue basting all vertical seams in the exposed quilting area, which will prevent the layers from shifting horizontally from the motion of the hopping foot.

3. Stitch all the horizontal seams next in the exposed quilting area; then advance the quilt.

4. Again, stitch the verticals, stitch the horizontals, advance the quilt. Repeat until the entire quilt is basted.

Use the Greek Key threadpath to machine baste all the layers together. This is a great pattern to continuous machine baste in preparation for all types of quilting, from hand to machine quilting.

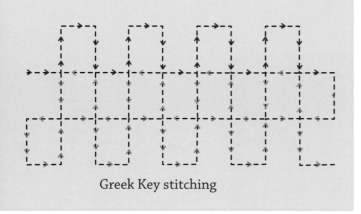

Greek Key stitching

OFF-CENTER BACKING

As you quilt, the quilt top must be centered on the backing from side-to-side but the top is offset from the backing top-to-bottom when loaded onto a frame/track machine with rollers.

Think of a magazine as representing the three layers of a quilt—the cover is the quilt top, the pages are the batting, and the back of the magazine is the backing. Now roll up the magazine to mimic rolling the quilt onto rollers. You can see how the take-up rollers will take up more backing and batting than the quilt top, because the quilt top rolls to the inside.

To allow for the difference, the upper edge of the quilt top is positioned higher, usually 1" from the batting and backing top edge.

Fold both the backing and quilt top in quarters. Stack them on top of one another, matching the folds and the center fold corner.

Make sure enough batting and backing extends beyond the borders—at least 3"–4". You want no less than 5" at the bottom when loaded on the machine.

If you are a traditional machine quilter, lay the backing wrong-side up on several tables pushed together (take advantage of your local quilt shop's classroom) or the floor. Tape the edges to the table, starting at a corner of the table and working out toward the other corners. The backing should be smooth and taut, not stretched.

Smooth the batting onto the backing, working from the corner of the table out then smooth the quilt top onto the batting, again from the corner out. Center the quilt top over the batting and backing. Before pinning, triangulate the quilt top by measuring from opposite corners with a metal contractor's measuring tape. When the measurements from the top right to the bottom left and the top left to the bottom right are equal, the quilt is square. In addition, you can use a right-angle cutting template to ensure you have right-angle corners.

Pin baste a fist-width apart across the surface of the quilt, working from the center out.

Triangulate again by measuring from corner to corner. When the two measurements are equal, the quilt is squared. Check once again after quilting.

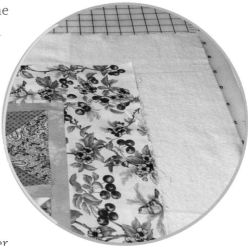

Batting extends beyond the borders.

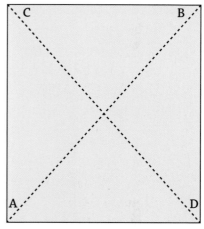

Line AB = 20"
Line CD = 20"
AB = CD   20" = 20"

Tip: When you are ready to load the quilt, measure the width of the quilt through the center, divide by 2, and that will tell you where to start pinning the corners to your leaders or zipper system to ensure a squared-up quilt. Mark your leaders or zippers in 1" increments from the center out, then pin the outer edges of the quilt top to the number that matches half the quilt dimension. Distribute the fabric evenly as you pin, making sure the center is lined up on the center mark of the leader or zipper.

Avoid Trouble from the Start

BORDERS WITH TOO MUCH FULLNESS

When border strips are simply sewn onto a quilt rather than measured and cut to size, there can be as much as 2"–3" extra fullness in each border. This can create a major problem for all machine quilters. What do you do with all that extra fabric?

It is a bit easier to take up extra fabric in the horizontal borders when they are loaded on the frame, since the quilting will take up much of the slack.

Tip: If one horizontal border is longer than the other, take small ¼" tucks in the longer border as you are pinning the quilt to the batting and backing, or the leaders, or zippers on frame machines. Be sure to pinch the fabric between and not on the piecing seams so you are not altering the overall look of the pattern. You can take up almost 2" with this method. Stitch along the tuck fold to create a mock piecing seam.

Tucks on the piecing seams would change the construction lines.

Take the tucks between the piecing seams.

ABOVE: GARDEN QUILT, detail. Made by Cozette Hebert, Stonefort, IL.

Excess fabric on vertical borders presents a different problem. It is almost impossible to quilt in that much extra fabric within the exposed area on the frame. Instead, increase the threadpath density. For example, add a central motif with close crosshatching around it to take up the extra fullness in the vertical borders, then quilt a suggestion of that design on the horizontal borders.

LEFT: MOUNTAINS I HAVE CLIMBED, detail. Full quilt on page 13.

MOUNTAINS I HAVE CLIMBED, 67" x 88". Made by Mary Sowell, Paducah, KY, and quilted by the author.

Quilt top made by the author with Ricky Tims' HARMONIC CONVERGENCE pattern

As a last resort, remove the borders, measure, and resew them.

Here is my favorite method for measuring unmitered borders. Lay the border strips directly under the middle of the quilt from top to bottom.

Cut two pieces the exact length of the quilt.

Sew onto the sides of the quilt. Then lay the remaining border strips under the middle of the quilt from side to side. Cut two pieces the exact width of the quilt and sew to the top and bottom. Your quilt is now square and there is no excess border fabric to ease.

FAILURE TO PLAN AHEAD

In our eagerness to get to the quilting, we sometimes sacrifice planning time. Not planning or marking the quilting patterns before the quilt is loaded tends to get us into lots of trouble. It can affect the spacing, pattern direction or angle of rotation, the space between patterns and free-motion designs, and your fills and meanders.

You can forget what pattern you put on the top border by the time you get to the bottom, as I did many times while free-motioning. Take a quick picture with your camera or phone. Consider printing it out. Trace over the stitching on translucent architectural vellum or a clear plastic sheet or film for future reference so you will not have to unroll the quilt back to the top border when you get to the bottom. You will have a clear record of what designs you used and which way you oriented them—facing in, facing out, or rotating.

Layout Design Sheet

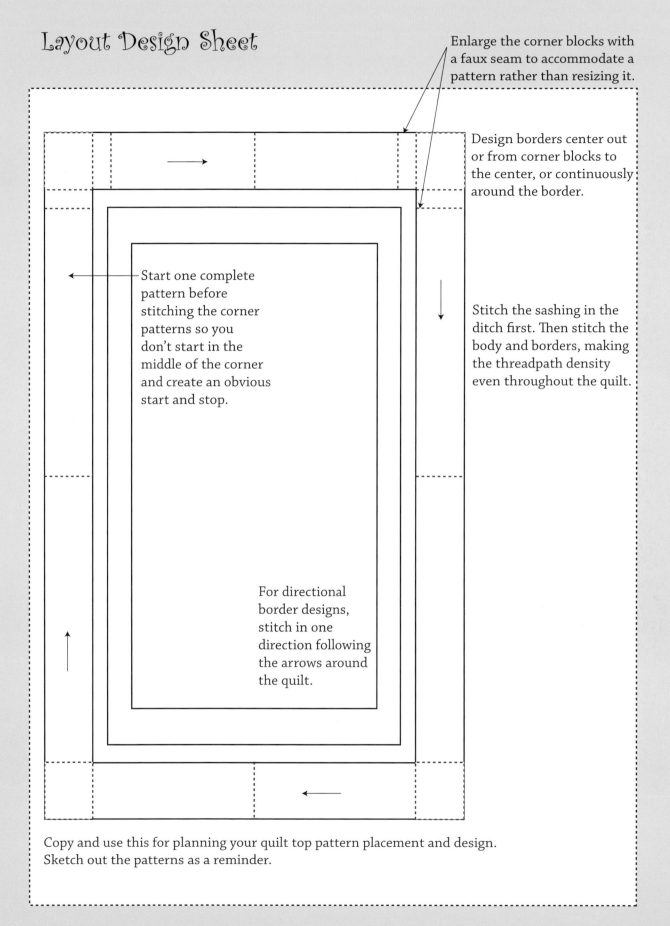

Enlarge the corner blocks with a faux seam to accommodate a pattern rather than resizing it.

Design borders center out or from corner blocks to the center, or continuously around the border.

Start one complete pattern before stitching the corner patterns so you don't start in the middle of the corner and create an obvious start and stop.

Stitch the sashing in the ditch first. Then stitch the body and borders, making the threadpath density even throughout the quilt.

For directional border designs, stitch in one direction following the arrows around the quilt.

Copy and use this for planning your quilt top pattern placement and design. Sketch out the patterns as a reminder.

NATURE'S FIREWORKS, 87½" x 89". Made by the author
with a wholecloth sunprint fabric from Langa Lapu Fabrics.

QUILTING PATTERN SELECTION

Not many of us design the quilt patterns before we start piecing the quilt, but often we'll think of designs during the construction. If you are like me, you may have lots of great ideas as you go along, but when you are ready to quilt, it may be weeks or months later and all your ideas may be forgotten.

Use a layout sheet (page 15) and sketch out your design ideas for future reference. Add your thoughts and possible patterns as they come to you until you are ready to load the quilt. How wide will you trim the edges? What binding sizes and styles will be appropriate? Do you want to use a special batting? Make notes of these decisions and more. Note thread choices and attach samples with a stapler or adhesive tape.

I punch my layout sheets and put them in a notebook or pin them to the quilt top. Even if I don't get to quilting it soon, I will still have the initial inspiration. Having all that information in one spot helps me remember how things were originally thought out.

Often I'll let a quilt top hang on a large plain wall using those wonderful pant hangers to clamp the fabric. I hang them on small cup hooks I've installed in the ceiling about 16" apart. As I continue to look at the quilt top, ideas come— if not this week, then maybe next week.

To get your creative juices flowing, try coming up with a name for your quilt. This quilt is a wholecloth stitched on Langa Lapu fabric from South Africa. I decided to hang it on the wall across from my machine where I could see it every day. Nothing really came to me until I suddenly had the urge to name it NATURE'S FIREWORKS (page 16). That was it—the name gave the designs a focus. (You may remember this quilt from the cover of my book *Pathways to Better Quilting.*)

By the time you actually get to quilting, you will have mentally quilted the top hundreds of times. It may become one of your quickest and best creations yet—guaranteed!

MARKING

We all know it is hard to mark a quilt once you have started quilting it. If you are fortunate enough to have huge cutting tables or the long table of a track machine, you have all sorts of space to mark designs. The problem comes from trying to mark while your quilt is pin basted or on the frame.

Tip: Use the extended base that enlarges the lower arm of your shortarm, midarm, or longarm machine as a table to rest a stencil while marking.

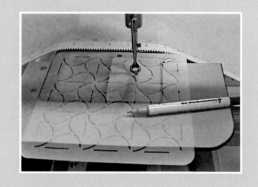

Avoid Trouble from the Start

If the fabric is light and not heavily patterned, you may be able to slip a pattern with dark lines right under the fabric even while it is loaded on the frame. Retrace and make the lines darker and more visible if necessary. Mark the design on the quilt top.

Pre-mark your quilt top

Stitching goes much faster when you mark all at once rather than continuously starting to quilt, stopping to mark, and quilting again.

Light tables are a great asset to marking. If you do not have one, open your dining room table and place a large pane of glass where the extra leaf would be. Then put a lamp underneath and you have a great light table. It's inexpensive and stores itself. What could be better?

Here is a great homemade light box. It is about 2' x 3' with holiday tube lights coiled up inside. The angle of the top Plexiglas® is perfect for tracing while standing or sitting.

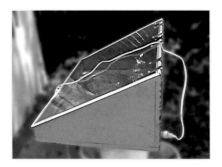

Audition patterns by tracing them onto page cover plastic, Press'n Seal® Wrap, or other transparent plastic or vinyl sheet. Lay the transparent copy over the quilt.

Color copy a quilt block and try out patterns on the photocopy. To see how your selected thread will look, stitch right on the printed paper.

RIGHT: **Seven fill patterns. Notice how nested Terry Twists create a secondary leaf design.**

Transferring patterns

Trace a quilting pattern onto architectural vellum or "thumbnail" paper (available at an architectural supply store) and pin it to the fabric. Stitch through the traced pattern at 8 stitches per inch. Tear away the vellum, pulling toward the stitching. The paper will release on both sides of the stitching at the same time.

Pin as many as 12 layers of vellum together, placing one drawn pattern on the top. Stitch the design through all layers with just your machine needle—no thread—on your traditional sewing machine. Pin or spray baste the needle-punched patterns to your fabric and follow the pattern of holes created by the needle. This is a great method because you can flip and rotate the design without retracing or making a separate pattern.

I will remove the thread from my longarm, pin a stack of vellum sheets to the top, and stitch. This saves me from having to go to my traditional machine.

Trace the pattern on tulle (wedding-veil netting) with a permanent marker, then trace over the tulle with chalk.

Tip: Do not use water- or air-soluble marker over permanent marker, since it can dissolve the permanent marker and take the ink into the fabric. This can also happen if you trace over permanent marker when marking through a stencil. Be sure to test before stitching light thread over permanent marker or pencil-marked vellum.

Removing blue water-soluble marker

I prefer to mark with a mechanical style chalk pencil and water-soluble markers. A caution about water-soluble markers: they can bleed through to the batting and migrate back to the top fabric. The biggest problem comes when laundry soap and blue marker mix, as the combination can cause brownish marks to reappear plus the heat of an iron will make them permanent. Be sure to rinse completed quilts twice in clear water before using soap to get rid of the blue marker for good—that is, one complete wash cycle without soap or detergent.

A light mist is all it takes to remove the blue water-soluble marker. Adding ½ teaspoon of baking soda for every 16 ounces of water seems to help. Keep a spray bottle of water and baking soda mixture handy and spritz the fabric after quilting an area to dissolve the blue marks. What a real morale booster when the blue lines are all gone. All the bobbles and wobbles disappear, too, and it looks like you really did follow the pattern outlines precisely, though we all know they are just a suggestion!

After spritzing, let the fabric dry enough to advance the quilt on the frame/table or lay the quilt on a bed. Since the quilt will become a little heavier from the water, be sure to distribute the weight evenly and let the quilt drape over curves and not a sharp table edge.

Removing mechanical chalk pencil marks

A Velcro®-style clothes brush will remove chalk markings. Just the handling of the quilt during the binding process can remove any remaining chalk.

Avoid Trouble from the Start

Tip: Quickly remove chalk marks with a small air compressor. The pressure of the air simply whisks it away. Store the compressor right under your frame/table so it is handy and remove the chalk as you work on your quilt top.

Some colors of chalk are harder to remove because of the colorant—pinks and purples, for instance. White chalk on dark fabrics will completely disappear. Be sure to test just in case.

UNEVENLY SPACED QUILTING MOTIFS

Pick patterns that are proportionate to the quilt sizes and leave margins proportionate to the quilt, baby to king. If you have a traditional machine or smaller throated machine mounted on a frame, then smaller patterns may be a good choice.

❉ Use patterns that can be divided into two lines of quilting for a larger overall design.

❉ Echo quilt around a smaller pattern to make it larger.

❉ Add additional shapes to a simple narrow design to increase the size.

❉ Break up long straight lines with "sprites"— recognizable patterns like a shell, flower, or basket motif.

❉ Use smaller medallion quilting designs sprinkled randomly across the quilt top instead of long pantos that require a lot of fabric manipulation.

❉ Use asymmetrical patterns that hide a lot of starts and stops.

RIGHT: Hooked feather variations

Avoid Trouble from the Start

❋ Line up patterns on seams with the Shadow Rhythms technique (pages 73–89), which creates a larger design with smaller well-positioned patterns.

❋ To position the patterns, mark the center of the block pattern or midpoint of the border pattern with a permanent marker on the paper (if tracing a paper pattern) or stencil. Mark the center of the block or midpoint of the border fabric with chalk or water-soluble pen. Position the pattern, lining up the center markings.

❋ Leave margins between the outermost edge of the pattern and the seam or piecing areas to feature and showcase the pattern.

❋ To get uniform positioning away from the seam lines, use appropriate widths of low-tack masking or painter's tape along seam edges. Luckily, it will not harm the needle if you happen to catch some of the tape as you zip through the quilting process.

TOO MANY PATTERNS TO BE MARKED

To avoid extensive marking, build a repertoire of free-motion patterns that you can stitch well without marking. Be sure to include coordinating designs that look good as small-, medium-, and large-scale designs. Choose sets of three patterns from among the patterns, stencils, and templates you have on hand that coordinate well together—for example, feathers, ribbon fills, and parallel lines.

They will supply you with easy "go-to" patterns for everything from tiny fill areas to large borders. Take advantage of the timesaving Walking Borders technique (pages 54–72).

RIGHT: MOUNTAINS I HAVE CLIMBED, detail. Full quilt on page 13. Notice how the patterns on the seam create an interesting negative space center design.

Pathways from **Quilt Top** to **Quilted** by Sally Terry

Avoid Trouble from the Start

QUILT THEMES AND QUILTING STYLES

Do everything you can to use the right style patterns for each quilt. You probably already have some favorite stand-by patterns in your repertoire that work well together and can be used on many different styles of quilts. Use this list of quilt styles and appropriate quilting designs as inspiration for creating sets of go-to designs.

Amish—simple feather design and wreaths, parallel lines, matching thread colors

Animal—casual, variegated thread, write animal sounds over top

Aztec—geometric and repetitive, suns, primitive, serpentine

Casual—informal, fun, spirals, straight lines, variegated thread

Civil War—feathers, feather wreaths, crosshatching, background ribbon fill, Baptist Fan

Charm—allover design with beige thread or coordinating variegated thread

Contemporary—allover design, variegated thread, geometric, simple large shapes

Country—flowers, leaves, feathers, outlining, earthy tones of thread, Baptist Fan

Country French—yellow, blue, white, red colors; flowers, paisley shapes, parallel lines, open patterns, dense fills

Children—anything fun, images, bright variegated threads, circles, loops, hearts, butterflies, bugs, write in names, dates, and giver

Cottage—casual and elegant at the same time, Baptist Fan

Dorm—big patterns, variegated thread, student's name, utility quilting and binding

Floral—leaves, flowers, ribbons, elegant meander, feathers, parallel lines

Memory—stitch in the ditch, outlining, allover meander, variegated thread, design theme of hobbies or interests

LEFT AND OPPOSITE: MOUNTAIN CLIMBERS, detail. Full quilt on page 80.

Novelty—fun, casual, bright thread, undulating lines, casual theme designs

Patriotic—stars, fireworks, outlining, ribbons, swags, flags, red-white-and-blue variegated thread

Primitive—casual, simple shapes, outlining, background fills, stylized quilting designs

Scrappy—allover, variegated thread or beige thread, edge-to-edge meanders

Southwest—spirals, undulating squiggles, tribal images, variegated thread, serpentine

Sports—balls, bats, helmets, gloves, shoes, star meander, team color thread

T-Shirt—allover meander fitting theme, school, sports; write in names, dates, circle special team names, schools, emblems, numbers, etc.

LOADING ON THE FRAME

When loading a quilt onto the frame, you want the greatest amount of the quilt top exposed either horizontally or vertically to cut down on the number of times you have to advance the quilt.

It can be very difficult to avoid skewing a directional pattern if it's quilted horizontally instead of vertically, so review the pattern layout. If the quilt is a wallhanging or will be displayed in a certain direction, make sure the patterns are positioned correctly—trees growing up, not lying on their sides, for example. The same goes for hearts and directional flower patterns. If the difficulty of quilting the directional pattern outweighs the advantages of fewer advances, load the quilt so you can quilt the pattern with the true top of the image at the top of the quilt.

AWKWARD SPACES TO FILL

Find meander patterns that work well in odd spaces, like the ribbon meander, or use a free-motion design with plenty of swashes, curls, and flourishes to fill the awkward spaces. They will blend into the areas more easily and are compatible with many designs.

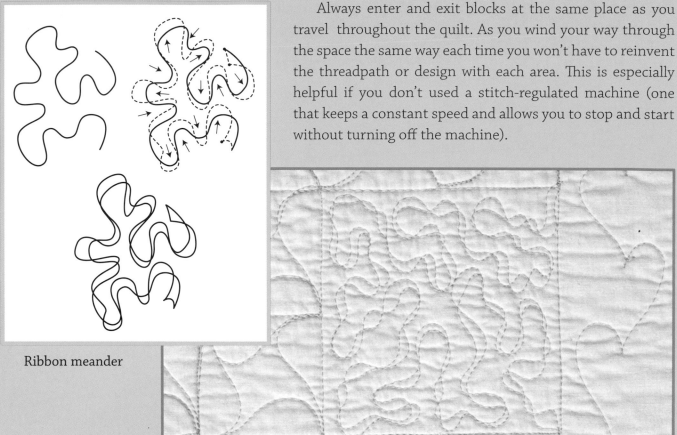

Ribbon meander

Always enter and exit blocks at the same place as you travel throughout the quilt. As you wind your way through the space the same way each time you won't have to reinvent the threadpath or design with each area. This is especially helpful if you don't used a stitch-regulated machine (one that keeps a constant speed and allows you to stop and start without turning off the machine).

RESIZING CHALLENGES

If you have a pattern whose design is perfect for your quilt but is too big or too small, you will need to resize the pattern. Divide the size you want by the size you have (using the length or width measurement), then multiply by 100 to get the percentage of increase or decrease for a copier. A proportional scale (shown at right; available at quilt and craft shops) will take the math out of your calculations. Simply line up the two sizes and the percentage of increase or decrease will be shown.

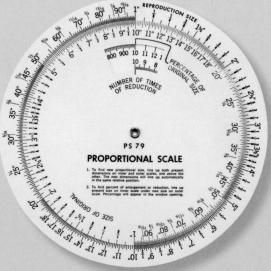

Reducing patterns, or even stencils, on a copier can introduce inaccuracies; be sure to measure after every copy. If you need to reduce or enlarge again, measure again, since the percentages will change each time.

Go to **www.quiltscomplete.com** and click on the calculator page to find out how many rows, how far from the upper and bottom borders, and how far apart to position a pantograph. This is a real timesaver. Be sure to bookmark this site in your browser.

Resize pantograph designs by placing one repeat in the copier, print out the corrected size, then reprint the new size and tape together several reprints to make the needed length of the pantograph.

Measuring without measuring

1. Take a strip of calculator/adding machine paper the length of the area to be quilted.

2. Fold the strip into quarters or thirds—whatever division is appropriate to the area being quilted.

3. Snip the corners for easy alignment. The notches will act as registration marks.

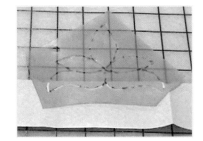

4. Use the measurement of the distance between the notches to find a pattern among those you already have on hand that will fit the space so you don't have to redraft or resize.

5. Mark the back of your track machine with tape or a marker at the notches to align panto patterns, Baptist Fans, or other designs.

Tip: If a design size fits perfectly along the top and bottom borders but not the sides, use an additional quilting design or motif in the center of the side borders to accommodate the difference.

6. Position a ruler diagonally across a space to equally divide it. Complete instructions are found in Appendix A of *Pathways to Better Quilting*.

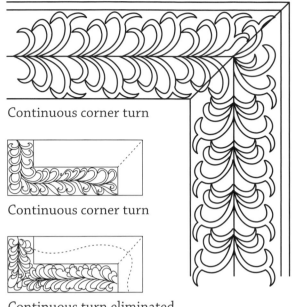

Continuous corner turn

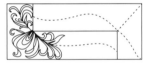

Continuous corner turn

Continuous turn eliminated

Continuous turn eliminated
with a separate corner design

TURNING BORDER CORNERS

Directional border patterns can be quilted continuously around a corner or you can stop them at a border corner block, eliminating turning the corner. This is especially helpful when a pattern needs drafting and marking. Start and stop the design with hearts, spirals, or leaf cluster designs, or use an element from the pattern or stencil itself.

Tip: If the pattern is too large for the corner block, stitch faux corner border seams to enlarge the area to fit the pattern. (See the Layout Design Sheet, page 15.)

Angle the border pattern spine at the inside corner of the corner block designs eliminating mirror images on the inside and outside curve.

Even if the border design is directional, you can quilt the right and left border designs as you come to them with each quilt advance. Just remember to alter the direction as the pattern rotates around the quilt top.

Tip: Quilt the pattern in the direction it flows, which may mean quilting from the top down on the right side border and from the bottom up on the left side border when the pattern direction flows to the right, rather than quilting it backwards from top to bottom. It will probably look smoother and more consistent with the other borders with fewer bobbles and wobbles. Add a free-motion shape to fill any spaces you missed.

LEFT: OUT OF THE BASKET, detail. Full quilt on page 27.

OUT OF THE BASKET, 48" x 48", made by Judy Ingram, Benton, KY, and quilted by the author.
Inspired by SHADOWBOX BASKETS by Sally Collins from *Mastering Precision Piecing*, C&T Publishing, 2006.

The sticky note shows the direction of the spine design.

Straight line corner designs eliminate corner turns.

If you are not able to nest repeats exactly, insert several compatible shapes, like hooks, ferns, curls, or ribbon in several random places around the border, even if you don't need them, so when it is time to nest the designs you can add a random shape to make the border fit exactly. It will look totally drafted and perfectly planned.

Use a sticky note with arrows to help you with the direction or lay a piece a tape with instructions written on it to the quilt top.

Here is an easy way to make a quick corner turn from a straight pattern. Cut a section of a panto or traced pattern on a 45-degree angle to form a corner pattern or place two right sides together and refold on a 45-degree angle for a corner turn pattern.

NOT ENOUGH TIME

There are occasions when there is not enough time to audition patterns and thread—the baby comes early, the party date gets moved up, other events interfere with your quilting time, and so on.

Be sure to have your go-to-in-a-pinch patterns ready. If not, then simply present the quilt top and do the quilting later, after the wedding guest signatures, the birthday celebration, or the baby shower. So much time, handwork, and fabric are invested in the quilt top that we do not need to surrender good design and quality machine quilting and bring down the overall value of the completed quilt.

Promise you will find a way to get it done with style.

ZIGS ZAGS I, 37" x 52", made by the author. Part of an original jelly roll pattern series by the author.

Nuts and Bolts

WORKING WITH TEMPLATES

One-quarter inch thick Plexiglas templates make quilting shapes and outlines with a longarm machine easy.

Mark directly on the template or use low tack painter's tape to show margins and dimensions to help line it up on the fabric seams if not already etched in.

Use tape on the template to show where to position a portion of the template for quilting in special areas. Use piecer's ruler tape to mark areas on the template if you are only using a section of it, and for exact placement of repeats, starts, and stops. The tape (see Resources, page 108) is available in different colors and is slightly tacky, translucent, and repositionable. Make notes on the tape in pencil.

Keep thumb and forefinger on the template and your middle finger up against the template edge for better positioning and accuracy. Gently push the template against the hopping foot with one hand and pull the hopping foot against the template with the other hand for accurate stitching.

Spray the back with fabric adhesive to prevent templates from sliding due to the pressure of the machine foot. Remove build-up of fibers in the adhesive with water or alcohol.

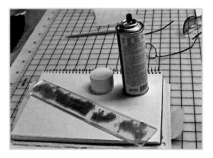

LEFT: DOUBLE DUTCH SQUARED, detail. Full quilt on page 37.

Pathways from **Quilt Top** to **Quilted** by Sally Terry

Move your hand along larger templates as you are quilting for better control, as you would when rotary cutting fabric with a long ruler.

Sometimes I will actually break a template into smaller pieces if it is too cumbersome to hold on the quilt top.

> **Tip:** Because the larger templates are hard to hold in place, first, make sure they are lined up correctly. Then mark the outer edges of the template right on the quilt top with chalk or a water-soluble marker to use as registration marks. If the template moves as you are machine quilting, you will be able to reposition it as you stitch, so your design stays accurate and does not angle off where you do not want it to go. This little technique will keep your patterns lined up perfectly.

For quilting on a traditional sit-down machine, trace around the templates to mark shapes on the quilt top.

TRAVELING THROUGH A QUILT TOP

Enter and exit the same place in each defined stitching area for continuous stitching. Since the position of the shapes is usually rotated around a block, it should be easy to see where you can travel between points and seam intersections or travel down a seam to get to the next area without breaking your thread. You may want to single stitch through intersections for a cleaner look. This helps keep the threadpath density and design uniform and you will not be "reinventing the wheel" with a brand new pattern path each time you fill an area.

> **Tip:** Mark a suggestion of your thread-paths from beginning to end. Try to stitch them all in the same day. Your brain often-times will forget from one day to the next how you traveled and your patterns and even threadpath density will not be the same.

If you need more control, create shapes within shapes to follow and fill. For example, follow shapes of letters (page 83). You can divide up the area into rectangles, triangles, or other shapes, then work to fill them individually until the entire space is completely quilted (page 32).

Here is a practice tip for determining threadpath directions in and out of areas. Practice a ribbon fill or any fill or meander pattern on a large white board or practice piece. Draw in piecing shapes other than squares that are commonly found in patterns. Work your way through the areas created by those shapes, filling it with your ribbon meander. Hold the white board flat, and hold the dry erase marker the same way you hold the handles on your machine or move your fabric under the needle on a traditional machine.

Developing good hand-eye coordination while moving your arms and holding your hands in the correct position will transfer to your

Nuts and Bolts

ABOVE: Using 3 shapes–loop, s-curve, and straight line—as a fill, lining up the points

RIGHT: Using all 5 shapes—loop, s-curve, straight line, hook, and arc—forming shapes within the fill

machine work. The brain does not know if you are at your machine or drawing on a white board as you build valuable muscle memory for each shape of the Language of Quilting. It just knows you're practicing.

Another practice tip: Choose 3 of the 5 basic shapes of the Language of Quilting for an overall meander. Repeat a shape 3 or more times, then stitch multiples of the next shape, and so on, filling the area. Try the same exercise using all 5 of the basic shapes.

HOW TO CHOOSE THE PERFECT PATTERN

The majority of quilts call for three areas of quilting—blocks, borders, and fill. Here is a quick and easy way to find the right designs in seconds, not minutes.

For me, choosing quilting patterns for a quilt is like choosing the fabrics for the quilt blocks, sashings, and border. First you pick the focus fabric. From there you select the geometric, medium prints, small prints, and background fabrics.

The same is true for picking the coordinated quilting designs for a quilt top. Pick your focus pattern first. This is the one that you will feature and will be the most prominent. Then use it to select the rest of your designs.

1. Determine the main feature or focus of the quilt top. Is the fabric a real standout or is it the piecing? Select a main quilting pattern or use a design from the fabric itself to work with, keeping with the overall feel and style of the quilt top. Use feathers, leaves, and flowing designs with the more traditional quilts. Use the more casual shapes and pattern designs on theme and utility quilts.

The focus quilting pattern could be a stencil to mark, a free-motion meander, or a pantograph pattern.

2. Now look for the 5 shapes of the Language of Quilting in your focus quilting pattern. Which are the 2 or 3 most common shapes in the design—arcs, s-curves, straight lines, loops, or hooks? Use these shapes to coordinate the rest of your quilting designs.

3. Choose background fills, geometrics, medium and small patterns that all contain the same two or three common shapes, keeping the styles the same. Once you see the repetition of the shapes, your pattern choices will be easy to make.

4. Audition the patterns, placing them side by side. Here is where you will see that some patterns work well together and some don't. You can like or dislike pattern combinations and not even know why. Now you know! You know they will work together visually because they contain the same common shapes.

Now you will only be quilting those same 2 or 3 shapes throughout the quilt top as they combine to become roses, leaves, flowers, hearts, and vines. As long as the shape is pretty you don't have to rip out! It doesn't matter if it is slightly (or entirely!) different from what you originally intended. So repeat after me, "As long as the shape is pretty I don't have to rip out."

These two stencils have shapes in common. The focus pattern contains loops, arcs, and s-curves. The sashing pattern has arcs and loops. For the background fill simply choose one of the 3 shapes.

Stencils by StenSource International, Inc. and The Stencil Company.

HOW TO DEAL WITH MULTIPLE BORDERS

Multiple borders and sashings appear more and more often in quilt tops. With fabric manufacturers offering a greater number of colorways within their fabric lines, it is rare to see a single border. Sashings and borders vary in size, making machine quilting pattern

RIGHT: MORNING GARDEN, detail. Made by Ulla Shierhorn and quilted by the author.

Note the use of the panto design (page 35) on a very small scale instead of stitching in the ditch on the seam between the borders and the ribbon meander in the body of the quilt

Tip: On your colorful scrappy quilts, use a thread that blends with all the fabrics, like a "Mother Goose beige" or tan. White or ivory thread tends to look like string on multi-colored fabrics.

choices more complicated since they cross into different size areas with contrasting fabrics.

What color thread should I use? What patterns work the best? How can I quilt these multiple borders quickly and easily without changing thread and using a separate pattern in each?

Quilting each border separately can be very time consuming with thread and pattern changes. If you stitch one color of thread over multiple borders, patterns will "blink" as the thread blends in with some fabrics and contrasts with others. You lose part of the pattern in some areas while it stands out in others.

Variegated threads work well because they show in all the contrasting fabrics and will probably be your best choice for visibility as well. Be sure to look for threads that have color changes every 2"–6" to ensure that you will see the design across the different contrasting fabrics of the quilt.

Tip: If you're quilting with variegated thread, choose bobbin thread that matches the background fabric of the quilt top. Alternatively, choose a warm color bobbin thread for warm variegateds or a cool color bobbin thread for cool variegateds, a shade darker than the background fabric. For fabrics called "brights" with bright colors on a black background, use black bobbin thread. The darker bobbin thread showing on top will look like a hole, defining the stitching.

When working with stencils and templates, the patterns are typically lined up on a center line. With multiple borders use the seams between the borders as your center spine or center line, adapting to the different sashing/border widths as you go, creating a distinctive design in each.

Use a main pattern on seam, and with each additional pass add a different design for each part of the multiple borders or sashings. That way you will be able to see a consistent design for each individual border/sashing and an overall pattern as well.

For example, here is the little Terry Twist® panto. It appears as half a heart lying on its side, lined up on a center line, which could just as well be a seam.

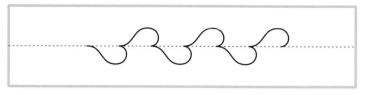

Terry Twist panto

Tip: This design is easy to adjust to the different fabric widths. It uses the Walking Borders technique introduced on page 54. Select from the 5 Basic Shapes of the Language of Quilting to add to the design, making each area different.

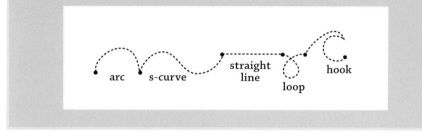

By treating each sashing/ border width separately you can quilt up to three different sashings or borders in one or two passes. What could be more fun? Each separate sashing or border will have a different variation of the pattern without any "blinking" where you lose the effect of the design

RIGHT: **Three different borders quilted with two passes, each based on the Terry Twist panto design shown above**

Marking Techniques

WORKING WITH STENCILS

On all of your stencils, mark the center, and the highest and lowest points. Try to find stencils that have the corner turn included, but if not, mark corner turn diagonals as well.

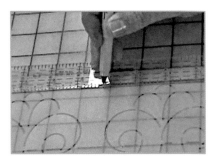

RIGHT: Mark the highest and lowest points of the pattern.

IMPORTANT: Use a permanent marker only where you will not touch the water-soluble or other marking pen as you mark through the cut out areas of the stencil. The permanent marker can be dissolved with water-soluble pens and transferred to the quilt fabric. (Ask me how I know!)

Extend the markings off the edge of the pattern or stencil to make it easier to align them correctly with seams or other positioning marks.

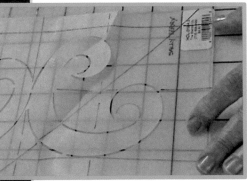

Extend the markings from the stencil to the quilt.

Do you have a stencil with a design you like but the shape doesn't work for the area you want to quilt? Create a new stencil by cutting it up, turning the pieces to change the configuration, and taping them back together for a better fit.

Making plastic stencils

Make a stencil of your own design with soft stencil material. It's usually blue in color and comes in rolls (see Resources, page 108). It is smooth on one side and rough on the other, with a pebble-like texture.

This flexible material is called DBK for double-blade knife. Normally you cut stencils with a double-blade knife, though I find that a single-blade craft knife works just as well. Even when I cut a custom, one-time stencil, I have always found a way to use it later on another quilt.

Mark the material with a permanent marker and cut, making sure you leave connecting bridges so the design does not fall out. Use a light-colored cutting mat or glass-topped light box underneath for the best visibility.

The rough side will help keep the stencil in place on the quilt top while marking with it, but I recommend placing it rough-side up when marking with a pounce pad. The texture will pull the chalk from the pad. Scrub across the stencil so the chalk will go into the fabric. Some quilters like using a sponge-type paint brush to really push the chalk into the fabric. There are also chalk markers and pounce powders that disappear with steam. Be sure to test first.

OPPOSITE AND RIGHT: DOUBLE DUTCH SQUARED, 41" x 41". Made by Heather Greene, Paducah, KY, and quilted by the author. PRETTY PAPERCUT pattern from *Fancy Feathered Friends for Quilters* by Susan Richardson McKelvey, American Quilter's Society, 2003.

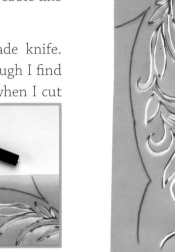

Stencil used to mark DOUBLE DUTCH SQUARED border (below and page 36)

Marking Techniques

Making cardboard stencils

In a hurry? A cardboard container like a pizza or cereal box will make a great stencil in a pinch. Here is a Terry Twist® pattern I created by cutting a cardboard stencil from a box and marking around it with a blue water-soluble marker. It held up beautifully and I can use it again on another quilt.

To make a cardboard stencil, trace a pattern onto architectural thumbnail paper.

Turn the paper over and retrace the design on the back.

Position the pattern right-side up on cardboard and trace over the original. The pencil lead on the back will transfer to the cardboard as it acts like carbon paper. Cut out the cardboard design.

Use the cut-out pattern to mark the pattern on your quilt.

LEFT AND OPPOSITE: PINWHEELS AND POSIES, details. Full quilt on page 72.

USING A SINGLE STENCIL MOTIF

Find the center of a block on the area to be quilted. Make a pin hole on the stencil beneath the selected quilting motif and line it up with the center of the block. Trace the motif, rotate the stencil around the center, and trace again. In a block area, trace each motif pointing toward the corners.

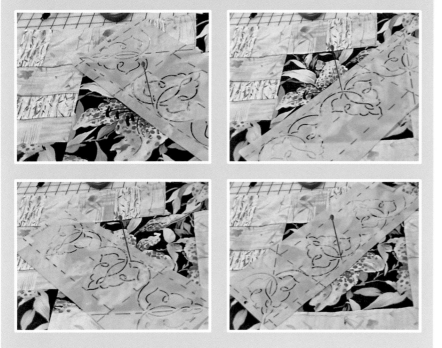

Place your centering square (page 50) under the stencil to line up the motif accurately.

TEAR-AWAY PAPER

Trace your actual-size pattern onto architectural thumbnail paper with a removable (not permanent) marker. Cut as many sheets as the number of patterns needed, up to about 12 layers. Pin the sheets together with the original pattern drawing on top.

Marking Techniques

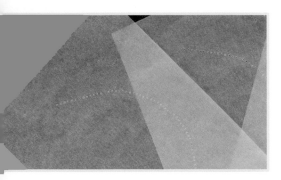

Stitch over the pattern on a traditional machine without thread, letting the needle punch holes to mark the pattern. You can also place a stack on top of a loaded quilt and punch with the unthreaded longarm needle.

Separate the sheets and pin the punched patterns to the quilt, saving the original. Quilt through the paper, following the needle holes.

Tear the paper toward the stitching to remove. It is amazing how cleanly it comes off no matter how small or large the stitches are sewn. The remaining side releases immediately, like magic.

If you need more patterns, use the original again. Only one tracing for multiple patterns! This method is perfect for custom designs, tracing around children's hands, following signatures, children's art work, copyright-free designs, and more.

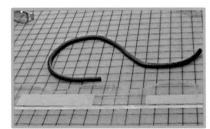

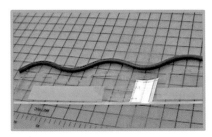

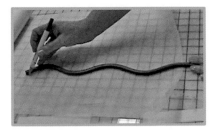

FLEXIBLE RULER

Flexible rulers come in various lengths up to 40" long. Bend them following a drafted or quilted spine or curve that you would like to repeat. The rulers hold the curved shape. They have a flat side that you can trace along with a small rotary wheel chalk or water-soluble marker.

Use your templates as a pattern and trace around their edges to form even more interesting patterns. Combine them with other templates and stencils, then transfer to your own stencil or to a paper pattern.

These are your tools. Mark them up and wash them off occasionally. Permanent marker comes off with alcohol. Some markings can be cleaned with soap and water. If your stencils are bent, lay them on a flat surface in the sunshine and let the heat of the sun work its magic to flatten them.

Loading for Quilting

LEADERS

Leaders—fabric or canvas pieces to which the batting, backing, and quilt top are attached—commonly stretch and bow out in the center where the pinning and rolling pressure most often occur. They need to stay in a straight line so as not to distort the quilt top during the machine quilting process.

Roll up all leaders so that the pinning edge is on top of the roller. Stand to the side of your machine and look down the top of the rollers to the opposite side. If the edge of the leaders is not lying in a straight line, tug the outer sides of the leaders at a 45-degree angle from the machine until they are squared up to the roller. Leaders need to be trained. Pull each one back into place after every quilt.

Occasionally lay a yardstick or carpenter's square across the leaders in the center to line up the centers of all the leaders. Work fabric back and forth until they line up again.

Mark the true center of all leaders by measuring from the outer edge of the metal or wood table frame using the same distance to mark each leader. Disregard the outer edges of the leaders as they all may be different because they roll unevenly back and forth across the rollers.

If you have zippers, then you may be able to zip the front leaders to the take-up roller leaders and roll them back and forth putting pressure on the leaders and squaring them back up.

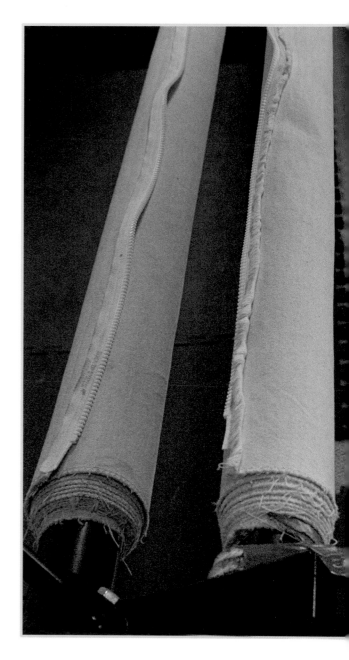

Loading for Quilting

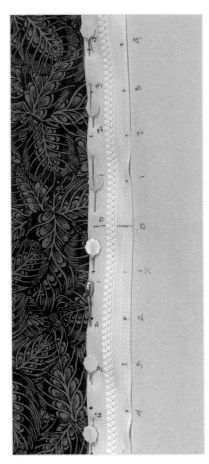

ABOVE AND OPPOSITE: **Quilt top by Ina Glick, Paducah, KY**

When purchasing zippers sets (Resources, page 108), purchase one set that includes both one for the leaders and one for the quilt, then get an additional quilt set or sets so you can pin several quilts for machine quilting at the same time. I recommend using large straight quilting pins and not safety pins because they are stiff and difficult to open and close, taking up valuable time.

Mark the leader for the bottom edge of the quilt in one-inch increments from the center out, starting with zero in the center. Tape a yard stick to the clamped leader and mark with a fine-tip magic marker all the way to the outer edge of the leaders. A 60" quilt top would be pinned with the center at zero and the edges at the 30" marks to the left and the right of center, squaring up your quilt top.

Pin the backing fabric from the center out without regard to inch measurement.

If you have zippers, zip them together first to find the true center and then mark the inches the same way from the center out so the markings align with the markings on the leaders. Mark the quilt set zippers for the quilt top bottom edge as well. It is not necessary to mark the inches on the backing zippers, just pin from the center out.

LOADING

Follow the manufacturer's directions for loading. Here are some additional tips:

✻ Directional quilt tops may need directional quilting patterns. It is nearly impossible to quilt patterns well when the design is rotated and lying on its side.

✻ Load most wallhangings with the top up since top and bottom borders are usually stitched with both designs oriented straight up and down. Side borders may be stitched directionally as well, with trees, for instance, standing up on both vertical borders.

✻ Non-directional quilts with non-directional patterns can be loaded lengthwise for minimum advances and maximum exposed quilting area.

✻ Fullness can always be reduced by using denser threadpath quilting patterns in the borders.

✻ Load a square quilt orienting the top of the quilt or directional fabric up.

✻ Load a rectangular quilt sideways with the top of the quilt to the left, unless it is a wall quilt or when the patterns are obviously directional.

❋ Orient a wall quilt batting with the least stretch lengthwise.

❋ If there is no sashing, stitch in the ditch between the border and body of the quilt for added stability.

❋ For odd-shaped quilt tops or tops with a scalloped or irregular edge, layer the quilt top over muslin and flat baste the two together ¼" from the edge. Then pin the muslin to the leaders.

❋ The center area of the quilt top is always the loosest and can be quite sloppy where it is pinned to the leader. Be sure to look underneath to see if the backing is sloppy as well. If the fullness is not taken up, tucks will appear in the backing, which can only be fixed by unstitching them. To prevent the tucks, tighten both the backing and quilt top fabric on bottom rollers and side clamps.

❋ Wedge a small roll of batting under the roller to take up some of the vertical fullness while quilting.

❋ Look at the straight horizontal piecing lines and be sure they line up in a straight line with a horizontal roller, tightening or loosening the fabric around the rollers when you roll up the quilt as needed.

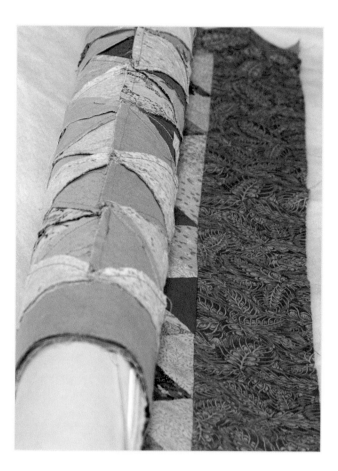

❋ If you will be turning the quilt to stitch the vertical borders in one long horizontal pass, turn the top clockwise. This will eliminate quilting fullness into a border/body seam and prevent creating puckers and tucks. All the fullness will be quilted out as the hopping foot travels from left to right pushing the air, batting, and backing away from already stitched seams.

❋ Fabric should float above the lower machine arm without seeing the silhouette of the lower arm through the fabric as you move the machine. Raise or lower the offending roller so you can just about put your finger between the fabric on the roller and the lower arm of the machine. Raise the same roller every two to three advances to eliminate drag from the layers of fabric rubbing against the lower arm of your machine.

❀ Too much fabric rolled around back and front rollers can also cause extended bases (large flat extensions that can increase the throat plate size to 10" x 10" or more) to drag. Don't forget to raise the rollers every two to three advances, if possible.

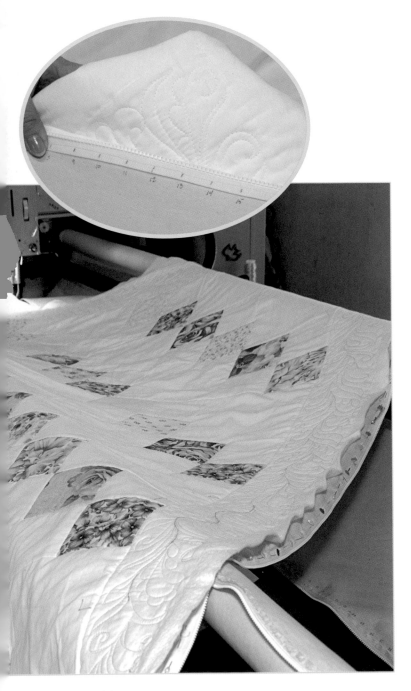

LOADING ON POINT

For quilts that need lots of diagonal quilting, like a Log Cabin Barn Raising configuration, reloading the quilt on point turns the diagonals into long horizontal paths for frame and table quilting. First pin the quilt on the leaders as usual. Complete as much of the quilting in a north/south, east/west orientation as you can. While quilting, baste the larger diagonal unquilted areas to be quilted on point, according to the batting manufacturer's maximum threadpath width recommendation.

If the quilt is a rectangle, fold it in half diagonally across the center from point to point. Lay the quilt on the front rollers and mark where you will be pinning the bottom corner to the leader. Rather than starting to pin in the center, the quilt will be offset because of the rectangular shape.

Pin in from the corner of the quilt top to the bottom leader along a 45-degree angle of a construction seam. Pin a minimum 10"–12" in length to provide stability to the quilt top while still lining it up correctly.

Measure the distance from the outer edge of the metal frame to the bottom point. This distance is measured from the opposite side to determine where to pin the top point to the leader.

Roll the quilt onto the bottom roller keeping the 45-degree angle seams lines aligned straight across the roller. Fold the corner of the quilt over onto the top so you can pin 10" to 12" of it to the leader. Since the patterns are usually quilted in the body of the quilt, the pinned point will not be quilted, so take up as much as you need to secure the quilt.

CLAMPING AND PINNING BACKING, BATTING, AND QUILT WHILE LOADED ON FRAME

Stay stitch down the sides of pieced borders before loading so construction seams do not pull out.

Pin first

Pin very flexible straight pins parallel to the quilt sides ¼" inside the raw outer edge through all three layers—top, batting, and backing. The pins should be bendable enough to roll around the take-up roller. This will keep borders clear of horizontal pins that can be in the way as you machine quilt the border pattern. You won't have to machine baste the edges, which I think can cause additional tucks and puckers if the borders are not measured and sewn correctly.

Remember, quilts can lose up to 2"–3" of the overall quilt dimensions, which will make up for irregularities in widths.

Pin from the center out to the horizontal rollers. To make sure the quilt is loaded squarely, measure in three places within the body of the quilt and get the average. Then pin to the average measurement and the top will square up during quilting.

> **Tip:** If sashing (or border) seams are pressed away from the sashing (or border), you will not need to change thread color as you are stitching them in the ditch.

Tuck or wedge extra batting under the rollers, pull the top to the sides with selvage strips, or place a weight such as a large round full can of veggies or bag of dried beans directly on fabric to ease fullness. I often walk my fingers pushing down on the fabric to the left of the hopping foot to take up the fabric while stitching.

Loading for Quilting

Wrap long selvage strips around the roller to pull and stabilize the edges of the quilt. Mark 1" increments and pull toward the quilt outer edge to make sure it is square on the rollers as you advance the quilt. Use a blue water-soluble marker to write notes on the selvage and erase when done.

Clamping

Clamp the batting and backing only along the sides (not the quilt top itself). As you begin to quilt you will also want to clamp the leader or zipper as shown. There are large clamps on the market that will pull the entire side evenly. Use long selvage strips tied to the side of your machine to hold or pull fabric into position. Be aware that pulling too tightly can cause distortion.

Fabric tension

Fabric tension should never distort the piecing lines of the top. As you sweep your fingertips across the entire width of the fabric, you should not feel it being pulled by the pins. Distortion from too much roller tension can actually be stitched into the top fabric. Either place the leader pins closer together, filling in the gaps, or release some of the roller tension.

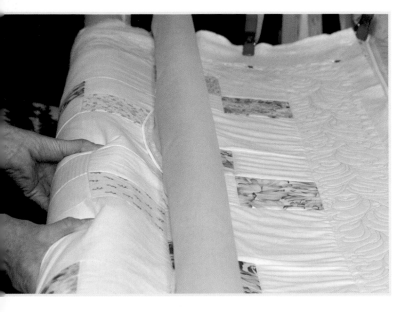

You can also back off some of the fabric so it is as loose as the surrounding fabric, then roll up all the loose fabric at one time. This is critical when you have too much fabric in the border. The borders should not sag and should be at the same tension as the body of the quilt.

Don't pull the fabric so tightly that you see piecing thread in the seams or that a square becomes a rectangle. I prefer the fabric to be a bit sloppy, not tight as a drum. If the fabric vibrates as the hopping foot passes over the fabric, then the pressure on the fabric is too great. This can cause skipped stitches. Release some of the tension and if your machine is adjusted correctly the skipped stitches will cease.

Skipped stitches can occur if you pull the fabric too tight when using a traditional sit-down machine as well.

Clipping threads

Clip visible stray threads that show through the top fabric. For loose threads dampen the fabric. Go through the fabric with a #1 steel crochet hook, grab the errant thread with a circular motion, and pull it out. Use a stiff long pin to move seam allowances or to hide dark fabric shadows under seam allowances. You may need to pin them in place until you have finished quilting that area.

Ideally you will take time during construction or pressing of the top to clip threads. If not, some machine rollers will expose the back of the quilt top so you can clip threads as you advance the quilt. Be very careful when clipping embroidery threads that you do not remove the knot. Fray Check™ sealant is your friend here.

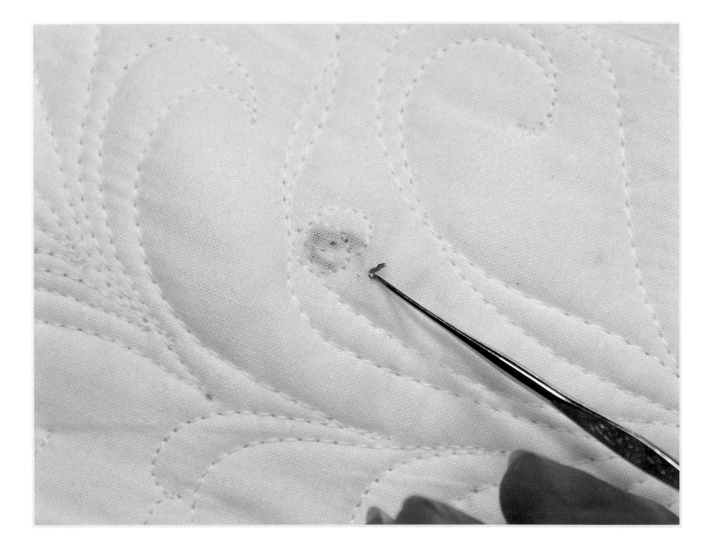

Quilting

ACHIEVING CONSISTENT THREADPATH DENSITY

Finding the perfect thread-path density is easy when you use the Rule of Thumb. That is, space your threadpaths on everything from feathers to block and border patterns a thumb's width apart.

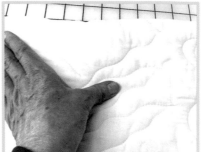

Tip: Lay your fingers down next to the stitching line and mark one, two, or three fingers away from your current threadpath for an easy, quick method of giving your quilt a consistent look and density. This works whether positioning stencils, free-motion designs, or pantographs.

For large meanders and other patterns on large quilts you may want to use the entire width of your hand (about 5") or make a fist and place it on the quilt top to space the patterns.

LEFT: PRECIOUS PANSIES, back detail. Full quilt on page 82. Features Shadow Rhythms fill (see page 73).

Remember to read the batting package for recommendations on maximum distance between stitching lines.

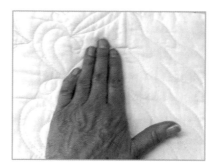

Tip: Using the width of your fingers works well if you are going to outline quilt or echo quilt. After all, that is how Hawaiian quilts are stitched. Woe be unto you if you gain or lose weight before your quilt is finished!

For small or tight patterns, use the foot on your machine to keep consistent threadpath distances. When the outside edge of the foot comes close to touching another threadpath, move in another direction. Focus on the outside of the foot as you sew, rather than on the needle.

Tip: Take art foam (available from craft supply stores) and cut 1", 1½", or even 2" diameter circles. Select the circle that is twice a big as the threadpath distance you want. Cut an X in the center and slip it over the free-motion or hopping foot on your machine and secure with a drop of fabric glue. Use the outer edge as a threadpath density guide. It will easily come off when you are done.

RIGHT: ZIGS ZAGS I, back detail. Full quilt on page 29. Features Walking Borders fill (see page 54).

Quilting

Make a centering square to help position patterns on center. Use stencil material and draw concentric squares at 1" increments from the center out. Punch a hole in the center large enough to mark through.

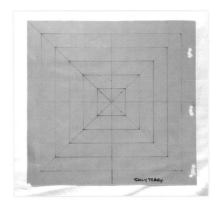

Position the marked square over your shape, block, setting triangle, or border, aligning the marked lines with the seams,

then mark the center through the hole. Center the vertical outer edges of the area first, then the horizontal. I keep my centering square near my machine at all times.

Most of the time we set up paper patterns, stencils, and template designs using the center line. For easy positioning, mark the center of the block pattern or center of a border pattern along with the corners and center of each side with permanent marker right on the paper pattern or on the stencil. You can even poke alignment holes in the stencil to mark directly on the fabric. Then mark the center of the block or border on the quilt top with chalk or water-soluble pen. Position the pattern by aligning the center marks.

MEANDERING: CIRCLES AND RIBBONS

Circles fit well in all the little odd angles and around appliqué and embroidery, whether at a small, medium, or large scale. Stitch about a half-inch of very small circles next to an appliqué, then enlarge the circles to fill the remaining area. What is extremely difficult is to have them line up in neat little rows. It would take hours of marking to keep the rows even and the circles consistent. I have seen quilts that started out with the circle background fill and by the time they got halfway through, the circles were different

LEFT: **Terry Twist** fill repeats the same motif.

sizes and no longer in neat little rows. Start out randomly, being consistently inconsistent, and you will be fine.

Turn a single-line meander into a ribbon by doubling back and weaving inside to outside and inside again. Be sure to leave room for the second stitching line as you're stitching the first. This is perfect around medallion centers and large appliqué as a background fill. It looks good whether small, medium, or large scale.

RIGHT: **Ribbon rose, quilted by a beginning student**

Tip: Make a large meander ribbon in a border, then fill in the areas between the ribbon curves with smaller, individual ribbons. Great when you need to take up extra fabric.

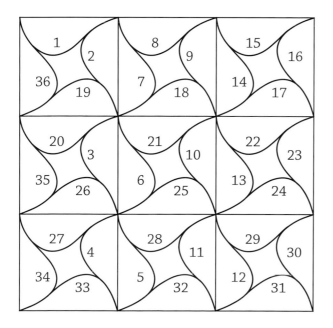

Use continuous-line patterns like the asymmetrical Terry Twist for quick, easy quilting as a background fill (see Resources, page 108). It works beautifully in randomly rotated large multiple squares and rectangle blocks because it adapts to different shapes quickly and still looks consistent overall, tying the shapes together.

LEFT: **Terry Twist—Follow the numbered sequence so each stroke is made exactly the same way.**

Terry Twist fill with a different design on each side

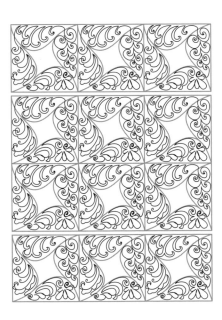

OPPOSITE: Quilted samples featuring the Terry Twist. Made by the author.

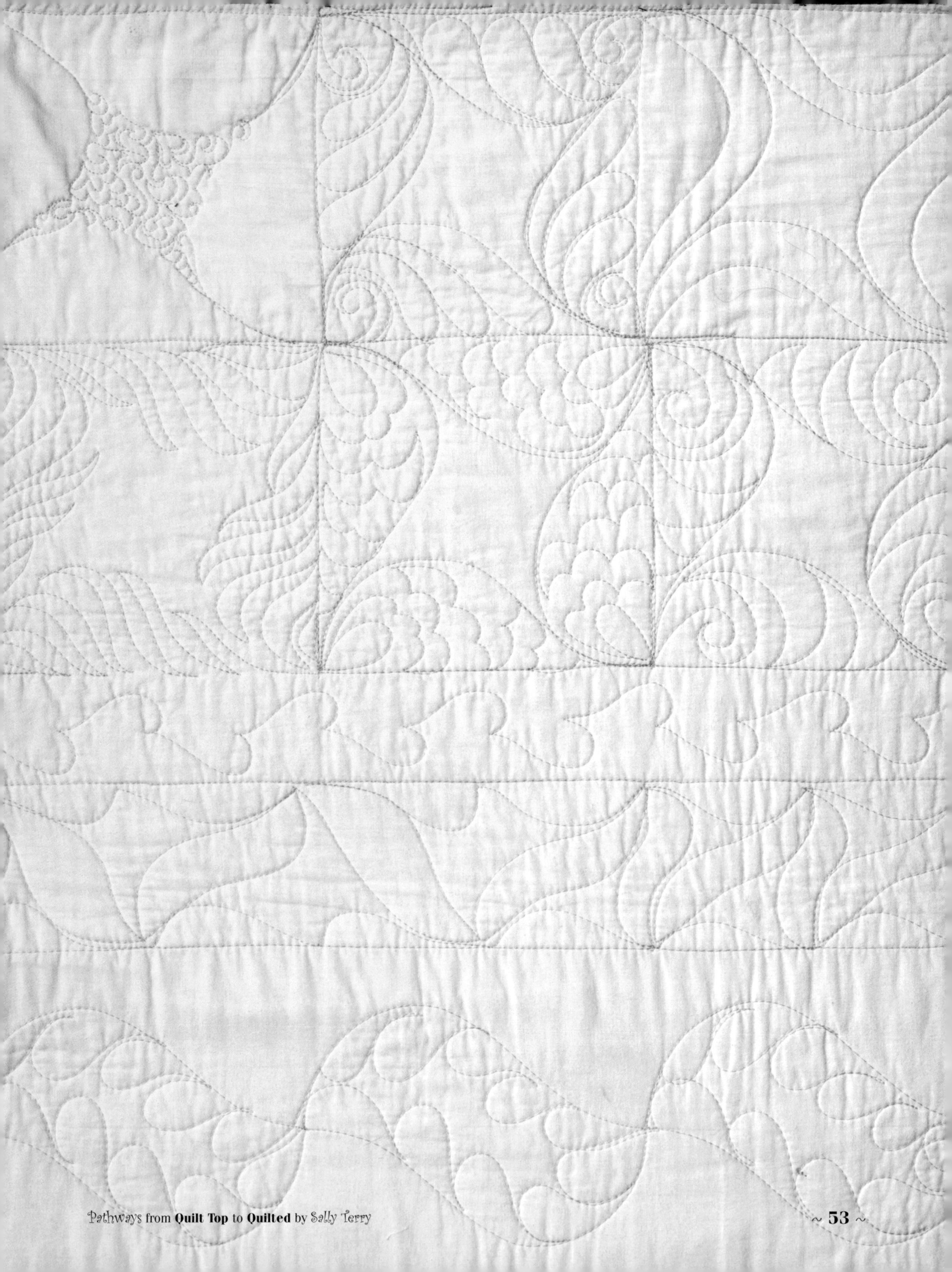

Walking Borders

The Walking Borders technique is an easy no-mark method that is quick to stitch with exquisite results. It involves stitching shapes off a seam or marked spine at a 45-degree angle. The spine itself need not be stitched, but rather is created by the free-motion movement of stitching the shapes on either side of it.

Continuous-line quilting is fast and friendly for borders, blocks, sashing, and edge-to-edge or large meanders. If you want to "load and go," this little technique will become a favorite. It's successful on all types of machines and even those new to free-motion quilting will love it.

- ❋ Use this technique with a meandered spine; it's perfect for heavily patterned borders and fabrics.

- ❋ Create free-motion, edge-to-edge or random stand-alone medallion quilting patterns instantly.

- ❋ Use on troublesome asymmetrical block shapes and large areas; quickly turn two-pass patterns into one-pass patterns.

- ❋ Adapt stencil and template spine configurations while coordinating with the quilt top style and size.

- ❋ Eliminate mirrored patterns.

Traditional sit-down machine quilters will find this technique invaluable since you are quilting in smaller areas and are moving less fabric. Quilt each shape or design, scrunching up the quilt around the throat plate to take the weight of the quilt off the area being quilted.

LEFT: Quilted sample featuring the walking border. Made by the author.

WALKING BORDERS TECHNIQUE

Step 1

Master some very basic shapes for "walking" on each side of the seam or spine without marking that can be easily stitched almost without thinking. Use leaves, curls, tendrils, hooked feathers, traditional feathers, plumes, hearts, loops, or ribbons as you quilt along, alternating the placement of the shapes on each side of your spine or seam. As long as the shapes are pretty, you don't have to rip something out just because it varies a bit from the shapes around it.

Step 2

Determine your stitching path and direction. Mark a center spine if you're not stitching along a seam. This is for you to follow, but it will not be stitched separately.

> **Tip:** Use a template or feather or vine stencil to mark an undulating, meandered spine. Leave room to get in and out of the tight space inside the corner turn. Make sure you are not so far away from the spine, corner, or seam margin that you will have to distort the pattern to maintain a consistent threadpath density.

It is important to note that if you mark a consistent, repetitive shape from a stencil or template for your spine, then free-motion quilt the rest, the design will have a more uniform look that will appear marked. It gives a more professional, controlled look to the quilting while saving time from marking. Use highlighter tape to mark your template for easier positioning.

The spine is only marked, not stitched. As you "walk" on each side of it, the spine forms automatically.

> **Hint:** Move the template against a border seam and stitch as a spine, then free-motion on the outer side into the border. Quilt constructed by Betty Lynn, Paducah, KY and quilted by the author.

Walking Borders

Step 3

Use recognizable shapes—heart, bird, leaf, etc.—as start and stop designs. Stitch the starting shape first, then the Walking Border design, then finish with the ending shape.

Step 4

"Walk" your design along the marked spine or seam, alternating on either side of the spine. If the design will go around the entire border or sashing as one continuous, directional pattern, build in "wiggle room" by adding a swash, flourish, tendril, or curl occasionally so when you finish, you can join the design by adding a swash, flourish, tendril, or curl if the patterns don't nest to your liking.

Angling shapes about 45 degrees as you alternately walk off the seam or marked spine makes for smooth, graceful patterns. This design is worked from the spine to the outside.

Design is worked from the inside to the outside.

Other designs are worked from the outside toward the spine.

Design is worked from the outside to the inside.

Notice the shapes do not touch but are spaced about ¼"–½" apart as the forms nest. You may have one large shape on one side of the spine and stitch two or three smaller shapes on the other side. This works well when tying to fill awkward pieced areas, while going around curves, or on corners and sashings.

Walking Borders

Play with center shapes along the spine. Keeping the center shapes consistent will mask differences in the outer shapes as you turn corners or fill different shaped spaces.

WALKING BORDERS VARIATION

The Half-Way Back Walking Borders variation works well for narrow pieced areas, sashings, and borders.

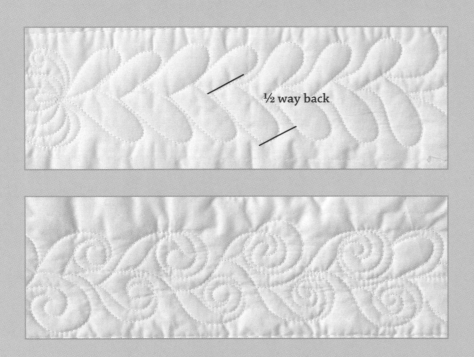

½ way back

Use a seam or mark a center spine. Mark the outer margins with a dashed line or low tack painter's tape. Begin in a seam or with a starter shape.

Stitch the same shape on opposite sides of the center line, finishing the form by touching "half-way" between the widest part of the previous shape and its end point. This technique looks better with one consistent shape or two alternating shapes.

REPETITION AND SEQUENCE

Using one shape

Alternate one shape in size from big to small or small to big in sequence or randomly. This works well for very busy areas with intense colors and patterns.

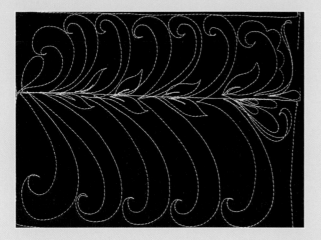

Add interest to a one-shape design with center motifs.

Using two shapes

Choose two shapes that are the same size. Walk on each side of the spine alternating the shapes or use one shape on one side of the spine and the second shape on the other.

Try using two or more patterns where your stitches are highly visible. Using a seam as a spine saves marking time.

Notice one shape on one side and alternating shapes on the other.

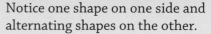

Using three or five shapes

Use three or all five of the basic shapes in sequence. Odd numbers help in alternating the designs. They appear more like a true marked pattern even though the design is entirely free-motion and unmarked. In addition, the same designs will not appear next to each other, which makes the results much prettier with a more custom look, and easier on you since you don't have to be perfect.

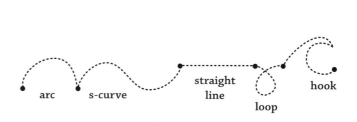

arc   s-curve   straight line   loop   hook

Walking Borders

Here 4 shapes are used in a group and alternated on each side in sequence. This works well on a guy's quilt.

Here are alternate sets of 5 shapes in sequence, repeated three times on each side of the marked seam.

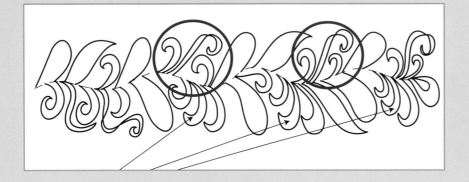

Here clusters of hooked feathers are used.

Using random shapes

Make up shapes as you go that complement the fabric and design tone of the quilt top. This works well in irregular spaces as the designs nest among the piecing areas, giving texture and movement to the quilt top. Use a curved or straight spine.

CORNER TURNS

Work your way around corners by repeating the same shape several times on the outside of the corner and eliminating some shapes on the inside of the corner.

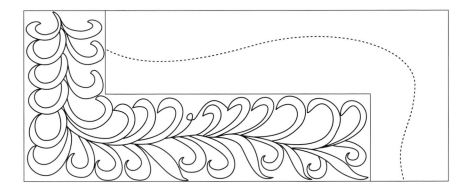

Refer to page 26 for corner turns and layouts. Mark or stitch a spine. Including random shapes will make a free-motion, unmarked corner look planned.

EDGE TO EDGE

Stitch on both sides of a marked edge-to-edge spine. Use large sweeping forms with a mix of small, medium, and large shapes so they will all nest together over the entire quilt top. Alternate the direction, creating beautiful, opposing negative areas between your rows.

You may want the spine to start in the body seam or use starter shapes and ending shapes. Since the curls, ribbons, leaves, and feathers are random, it is easy to fill up the spaces.

The more shapes you use, whether randomly or in a three- or five-shape sequence, the easier it is to nest the rows.

Stitch edge-to-edge. Keeping the designs at a 45-degree angle and a thumb's width apart will help them to nest.

MEDALLION TECHNIQUE

For smaller format machines and traditional sit-down machines, use the Medallion Technique to quickly fill smaller areas on a quilt. Medallions are simply stand-alone mini-Walking Borders stitched along a short seam or spine. Mark the spines over the entire top first.

For frame quilting, mark each area of the quilt as you advance the quilt or mark the entire quilt top before loading so you don't run out of room for the last medallions as you near the bottom border.

Mark large s-curves and arcs. Keep them on a 45-degree angle to each other. Use starter shapes of flourishes, ribbons, or more to begin stitching, nesting the forms into corners and the surrounding areas. Leave room between the spines for a starter shape so the medallion motifs nest.

For a more planned look use north/south then east/west positions; alternate them so the row underneath nests into the one above. Try an even more uniform layout with arcs in a scallop design or mark repetitive template or stencil spines.

Stitch by "walking" along both sides of the marked spine, stitching the shapes at a 45-degree angle to the spine, finishing with an ending shape. Keep the stitching lines a thumb's width apart as you nest the shapes with the surrounding medallions for consistent threadpath density.

Notice how the threadpath directions alternate instead of going in the same direction.

Smaller medallion shapes are great on baby quilts, florals, or any quilt that needs soft curving lines of stitching against straight piecing lines. Notice the starting and stopping shapes.

SALT-WATER-BED AQUARIUM, 76" x 93". Made by Janet Coen, Golconda, IL, and quilted by the author.
(See pattern credit on page 9.)

Walking Borders

Here the free-motion fish crisscross one another as they swim diagonally across the quilt top. I used an elliptical template for uniformity. This is the original sketch.

LEFT AND OPPOSITE: SALT-WATER-BED AQUARIUM, back detail. Full quilt on page 63.

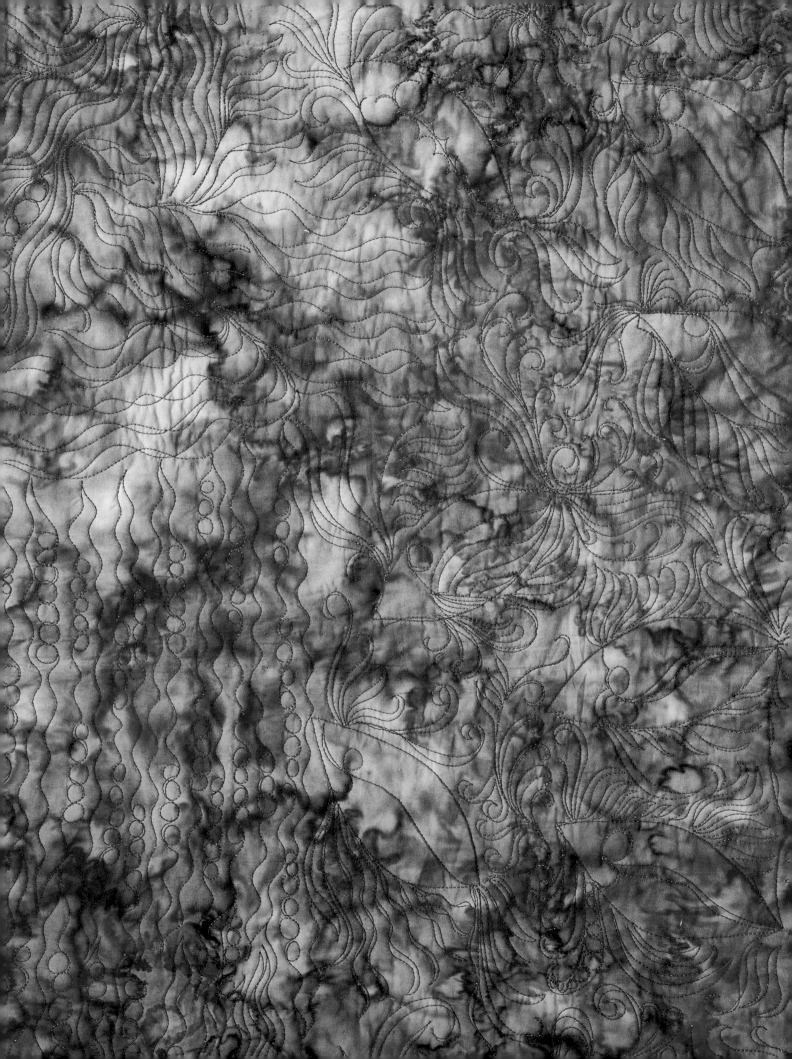

MEDALLION TECHNIQUE PRACTICE PAGE

Put in your starting shape, stitch by walking along both sides of the spine, and finish with your ending shape. Be sure to fill to the corners.

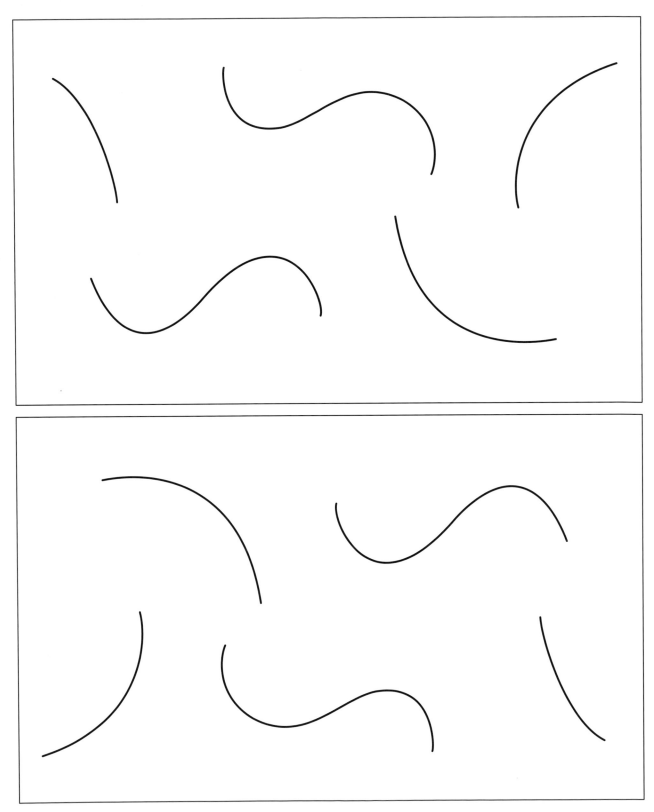

OPPOSITE: RIVER OF BALI, detail. Full quilt on page 68.

RIVER OF BALI, 71" x 90". Made by Nancy Wilson, Arlington, KY, and quilted by the author.
SNAKE RIVER LOG CABIN by Judy Martin in *Judy Martin's Log Cabin Quilt Book*, Crosley Griffith Publishing, 2007.

Instead of a spine or seam, try a walking border around a heart or other shape.

OVERALL MEANDER

Here is an example of one shape walking on either side of a marked meandering spine. Be sure to leave room to get in and out of tight areas by marking a center line in those areas, as shown by the dashed guide lines.

These tight-space guidelines could be to off-center, undulating, or centered as shown here. For larger areas, undulating guidelines would work well.

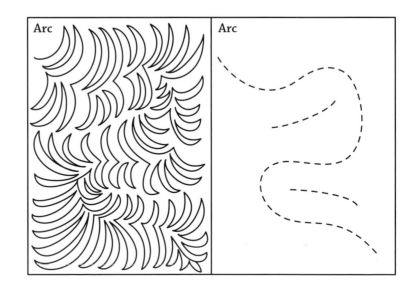

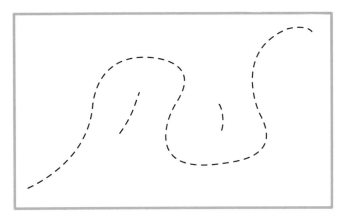

One shape can provide incredible texture around a meandering spine. Try one here.

Mountain Climbers, corner detail. Full quilt on page 80.

The Walking Borders technique easily turns corners without marking anything other than a curved spine. More and larger motifs are walked along the outside curve of the spine and smaller and fewer motifs are made on the inside.

This is fast and easy and coordinates with the free-motion meander quilting in the body of the quilt.

Sample of walking border easily turning the corner, made by the author.

Walking Borders

Here is another idea for you to try. Position motifs on the seam between the blocks instead of centering the design on the blocks. This frames the blocks with a single design and makes for quick positioning and creates an incredible overall texture. Notice how the pattern completes itself on the opposite side of a sashing, a large embroidered panel as shown, or even in a border. It gives the quilt top a look we are not used to seeing and adds interest and surprise. Try it!

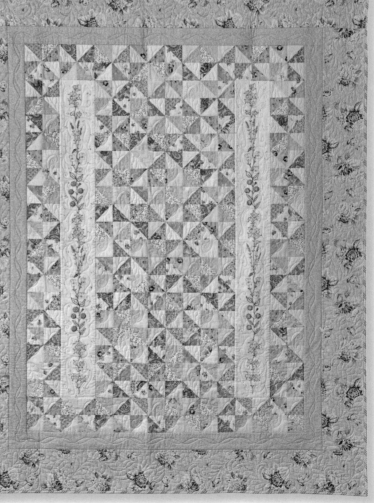

PINWHEELS AND POSIES, 67" x 84", and detail. Made by Heather Greene, Paducah, KY, and quilted by the author.
FRENCH COTTAGE GARDEN QUILT pattern by Meg Hawley, Crab Apple Hill.

Shadow Rhythms

Shadow Rhythms are closely repeated patterns that have both open unquilted (negative) areas and heavily stitched (positive) areas that create shadows across the surface of the quilt. It is a good technique for quilts where individual threadpaths would be obscured by complex piecing or heavily patterned fabrics.

The idea for this technique was a happy accident that stemmed from my doodling designs. The results are stunning.

Let's use the leaf shape as an example.

Create divisions following block or seam construction lines. Stitch the first area, then trace the design onto architectural thumbnail paper (see Resources, page 108). Lay it next to your quilting area to use as a pattern guide. The beauty of this quick technique is no marking. Simply count how many leaves you stitched in the first area and use your fingers to establish your spacing.

Notice how the close stitching, which builds up layers of thread between the leaves, adds shadows and defines the shapes.

ZIGS ZAGS II, details of back (above) and front (right). Full quilt on page 74.

ZIGS ZAGS II, 37" x 52", made by the author

Notice that the leaf pattern is different at all four points of the diamond, yet when combined they form an amazing unmarked pattern.

Shadow Rhythms

Here the designs are oriented facing up.

Notice how the design changes when the orientation alternates from row to row.

With just one little sketch, you can fill an entire area around a pieced center. The repetition creates depth and rhythm through the contrast of line and distance between threadpaths.

The right side of the pattern travels up along the shape to be quilted and adds movement to the quilt. This works well for setting blocks or for an all over, edge-to-edge fill for any shape block.

Shadow Rhythms

This is a directional pattern with one row facing up and the second row facing down.

The addition of curls, tendrils (a), and other design elements creates a horizontal line of larger leaves (b); the smaller leaves are created when the design is rotated 180 degrees every other row.

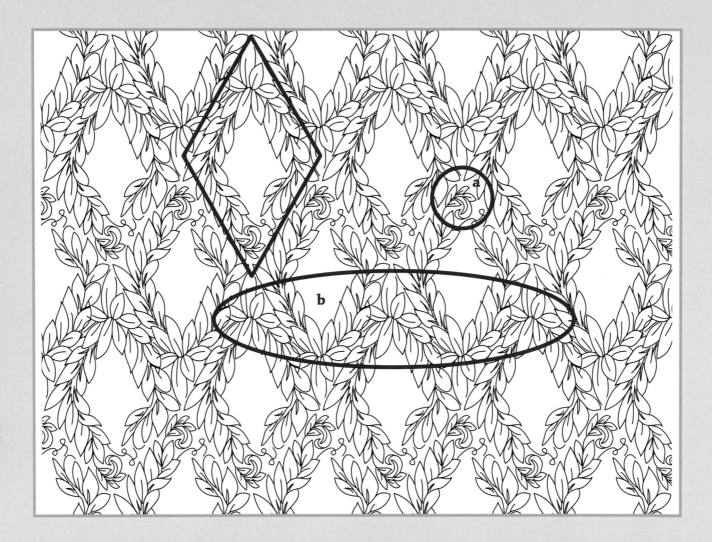

Notice that the leaves on the left side of the design are denser then on the right side creating the shadow rhythms. (Hold up the page at a distance and squint a bit to make this obvious.)

Start with one pattern to fit one side of an area, then reverse it to fill the entire space, leaving an open area of negative space to define the shapes.

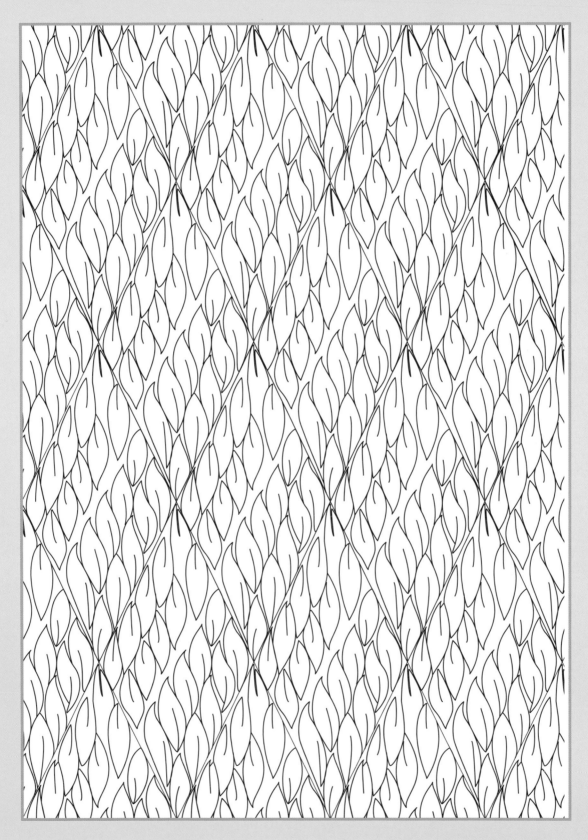

Shadow Rhythms

This pattern can radiate around a center point, stack up one on top of another, mirror repeat, and so on. Imagine this design done with variegated thread where you will not see much of the quilting and the rhythm of the shadows creates a visible star, heart, or other recognizable design.

- **1–2** Outline the leaf shape (page 81).
- **3–4** Stitch halfway into the shape and back to form a curved vein.
- **5–6** Stitch up to the tip and double back to the starting point, leaving a space between the threadpaths.
- **7** Fill the space with loops, keeping them perpendicular to the lines so they will easily follow the curve.
- **8** Double back along the loop-filled space to the starting point.
- **9** Travel to the next leaf.

Notice how the built up thread creates wonderful texture—the shadow of the Shadow Rhythms.

MOUNTAIN CLIMBERS, 45" x 45", and detail. Made by Heather Greene, Paducah, KY, and quilted by the author.

Adapted from MOUNTAIN MAJESTIES pattern designed by Bonnie K. Hunter, Quiltville.

Nest the shapes. Don't worry about inconsistent spaces in between. The spaces are what define the leaves and make the light and dark shadows of stitching. Travel by stitching two leaves, then create the next leaf between the two previous leaves.

PRECIOUS PANSIES, 86" x 98", made by Janet Coen, Golconda, IL, and quilted by the author.
Based on the pattern BREAKING OUT made by Maaike Bakker and Ineke Jongens from the book *Strip-Pieced Quilts,* ©2005 by
Maaike Bakker. Permission granted by Martingale and Company. 831 Baskets of K-Lace™ Criswell Embroidery & Design http://
www.k-lace.com.

DIVIDING SPACES

Divide blocks or areas with simple shapes such as arcs, s-curves, or straight lines. Letter shapes (C, I, O, U, V, X, Y) work well, too.

> Tip: If there is a lot of piecing and your dividing lines will not pass directly through the construction points, then make undulating lines instead of straight lines. This is a good technique to use when you want easy, unmarked quilting in an asymmetrical layout.

I have included the stitching sequence for you in the first example. Mark the spine to follow, remembering that the spine itself does not need to be stitched. Do the first block, count the number of motifs, then mark the spines and free-motion quilt the remaining blocks or areas, striving for the same number of motifs. It will look planned yet is much faster than marking the entire design.

Shadow Rhythms

Here are two shadow rhythm pattern layouts that adapt to large or small areas. The top pattern has a spine centered through the zigzag-shaped space. The lower one uses the area boundary or seam as the spine.

When dividing up spaces, look for elements that make up the overall pattern layout.

Consider the contrast between pattern sizes, light and shadow areas of stitching texture, and straight lines and curves.

This Log Cabin block is divided on a curved diagonal.

The block was pieced by Ina Glick, Paducah, KY, and quilted by the author.

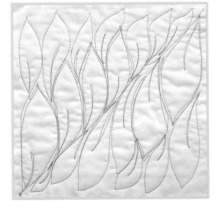

The design in the block corners will create a secondary design as they nest.

The block was pieced by Ina Glick, Paducah, KY, and quilted by the author.

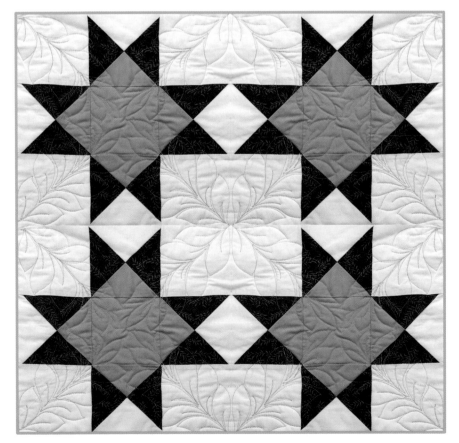

Shadow Rhythms

Look for balance of negative and positive areas and forms. You want balance of pattern sizes, threadpath density, and design across the entire quilt top.

Choose designs that relate to the pattern. Here the quilting follows the concentric piecing.

The block above was pieced by Ina Glick, Paducah, KY, and quilted by the author.

The block left was pieced by Janet Michaud, Vassalboro, ME, and quilted by the author.

The block pattern easily suggested an X pattern.

There is a starting cluster of leaves. The spine ends in an open circle. Rotate the starting point as the block pattern changes.

The blocks on this page were pieced by Ina Glick, Paducah, KY, and quilted by the author.

This strong directional design will help make irregular block designs and orientation more structured and less random.

The leaf pattern can fill an asymmetrical shape and continue in the sashing or border corner.

LEFT: PRECIOUS PANSIES, detail, made by Janet Coen, Golconda, IL, and quilted by the author. Full quilt and credit on page 82.

CORNER SPACES

See how well the leaf can fill corners—ideal for side setting triangles.

Use a template such as the Terry Twist to divide up spaces in large center blocks and the surrounding area with the same shape. For quick layout placements, if you follow the ⅓ : ⅔ proportions—⅔ of the space filled with quilting and ⅓ left unquilted—the design will be balanced and pleasing to the eye without a lot of planning, drafting, or marking.

EASY QUILTING PATTERNS FOR BEGINNERS

Don't be too hard on yourself if you cannot make certain shapes. Go with your strengths while learning. If you don't care for quilting hooks, leave them out until you naturally develop the skill to make them. It will happen. One day you will be quilting along and suddenly the pattern you could not stitch will be a breeze to execute. Cell memory and skills develop over time.

Learn one shape or technique a week. Don't push yourself. I took about three weeks to learn feathers. One week every quilt I machine quilted had loops, then one week it was hearts, the next week stars. You get the picture.

Note: Surprisingly, straight-line designs were the most difficult to learn. It took a long time to stiffen my wrists and arms, rock on my feet, and pause in the points and look where I wanted the needle or fabric to go. If I focused on pulling with my elbows, the seams were much straighter.

Use templates and mechanical motif making devices for threadpath perfection while learning to perfect your quilting shapes.

Choose patterns that look good in all different sizes for better overall design. Choose complementary patterns that contain the same shapes.

HOW NOT TO BE PERFECT WHILE LEARNING

Use asymmetrical patterns. Find patterns without mirror images. Constantly change the angle as you stitch the designs so they appear random. Be consistently inconsistent.

Cluster shapes into groups of small, medium, and large so that you're not committed to making same-size shapes.

HOW TO BE PERFECT WHILE LEARNING

Use templates or a mechanically guided stylus. Limit yourself to just three patterns per quilt—the ones you feel most comfortable with and do the best. Even though you use them repeatedly, scaling them small, medium, and large will give them a different look and feel.

As you stitch a pattern, make each of its component shapes of the Language of Quilting in one stroke. It will smooth out your lines dramatically. Use the machine foot to judge distances for more consistent spacing.

Count a rhythm as you execute each shape, much like you would count in time to music—the same number of counts per each of the same shape of the same size. Increase the count for larger shapes; decrease for smaller shapes.

Always look where you want to go, not at where you are or where you have been.

On a track machine, speed up your movements, quilt a bit faster, and throw the weight of the machine around. Throw it out there and let it come back using the natural arc of you arms. Combining this technique while executing each shape in one stroke will go a long way to perfecting your machine-quilting skills.

Backing, Borders, Batting, and Binding

BACKING

The backing center seam should be loaded on the table/frame parallel with the bars if possible. If the seams are perpendicular to the frame, layers and layers of seam allowances will pile up as the quilt is rolled, creating loose fabric on each side of the seam. This can result in quilting tucks into the fabric. When measuring for backing, consider how the quilt will be loaded and seam accordingly.

Press seams to one side so they are not open where the batting can beard through.

If the backing seams must be positioned perpendicular to the rollers, one solution is to gently nudge the seam allowance with one wrap to one side and the next wrap to the other side as you roll the back, eliminating layers on top of one another.

Consider back-art when you're positioning the backing to ensure it is aligned properly with the quilt top.

An unavoidable vertical backing seam down the middle should be hand tightened to prevent tucks as the backing is rolled around the backing roller.

Throw the backing fabric over another canvas roller and let the friction of the canvas put even resistance on the backing fabric as you roll it up on the backing roller.

LEFT: PRECIOUS PANSIES, detail, made by Janet Coen, Golconda, IL, and quilted by the author. Full quilt and credit on page 82.

Center the backing by finding the center of the sides of both the quilt top and backing. Place a pin at the center of the quilt and the backing. Then place small safety pins every 8" out from the center pin to the top edge of the quilt. When loading the quilt, position the quilt top an inch or two higher to allow for backing and batting fullness. Then try to line up the pins as you stitch to the center point. You will be close to the center point on the quilt top and the backing

Tip: When measuring for backing and batting, do not measure the quilt borders. They may stretch and not reflect the true dimensions of the quilt. Instead, measure several places through the middle of the quilt (both length and width), average the measurements, and add 8" to both the length and width. Use these measurements to determine how much backing and batting you need.

BORDERS

See the section on borders in the troubleshooting chapter (page 12).

BATTING

Use black batting on quilts with predominantly dark and black fabrics. Fabrics categorized as brights typically have black backgrounds with brilliant true color patterns. If you are adding any light or white embroidered panels, back them with the light fabric.

Tip: Grade dark seam allowances so they do not show through a light top fabric as a dark line or shadow.

Always load batting with its scrim, resin, or bonded side down, against the backing. (Note that some wools are heat bonded on both sides.) Scrim is a fine layer of polyester mesh adhered to the cotton batt that prevents the batting from being pushed through the back of the quilt by the needle. No doubt you have seen tiny little tufts of batting poking through the fabric because the batting was not placed scrim- or resin-side down.

If you are having trouble determining the scrim side, separate a corner of the batting. The scrim will easily peel away. For resin-coated batting, the resin side is smoother-looking but will feel rougher to the touch and it will glisten.

Notice the holes in the light layer of scrim.

On a needle-punched batting, look for little tufts of batting on the back side (backing side) as a result of the needling. Thousand of needles punch through the fibers from the top, meshing them together, pushing tiny puffs of batting, like pilling on a sweater. Needling also allows the sewing needle to pass through the layers more easily, especially for hand quilters.

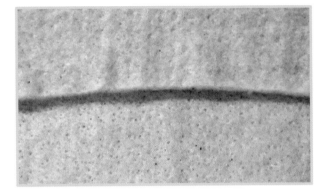

Load the batting with the pilling side down, and the direction of the needling will be the same as the direction of your machine needle as it goes through the batting. Look very closely at the batting and you will be able to see the needling holes are bigger on the top side where the needles went in and smaller on the pilling side where they came out. The larger-hole side should be up and the tufts down toward your backing fabric.

Batting also has a grain. One direction will stretch more than the other, just like fabric. If the quilt will hang, position the less stretchy grain vertically to prevent sagging and add stability to the finished quilt.

If doubling up batting, put the bottom batting scrim down and the top batting scrim up. If worried about bearding, use a fine layer of cheesecloth between the batting and quilt top. Few batts today require prewashing, but if you choose to wash your batting, follow the manufacturer's instructions. Use caution with a washing machine as the fibers can clog it.

If not smoothed before loading, the folds resulting from tight packaging can easily be quilted in as tucks that are hard to remove without unstitching. Fluff cotton batting in the dryer on low for several minutes to remove the wrinkles. Air fluff poly batting or take the batting out of its package and let it relax by spreading it out over the machine table or flat surface the day before you start quilting. You may even want to mist it with plain water to help it relax.

Cut two 10" squares from a variety of batting types, layer with the same top and backing fabrics, and quilt them using the same quilting pattern. Be sure to write the batting type on the squares with a permanent marker. Sew the squares together in two sets. Wash one set and leave the other unwashed so you can see how the battings behave both before and after washing.

This is a good project for a group of guild members, each one making sample squares of one type of batting, then exchanging them so that everyone has her own set of samples.

Fairfield Machine 60/40 Blend® Batting

Hobb's Poly-Down® Polyester

Matilda's Own cotton/wool w/scrim

Quilters Dream Select Poly

Matilda's Own 100% wool

Hobbs Heirloom® Natural with Scrim [100% cotton w/scrim]

Note: We used the same pattern for all samples so the differences are noticeable.

Warm & White® Cotton Batting

Hobbs Heirloom® 80/20 Cotton Blend

If the quilt is a gift, include a portion of the batting packaging that contains the washing instructions.

BINDING

Use bias binding for curved borders, angles, and quilts that will receive a lot of use such as utility and kids' quilts. As the edges wear they will not fray. Cutting striped fabric on the bias creates wonderful diagonal binding designs that really enhance your quilts.

Use narrower binding cut about 1¾" on the grain with mitered seams for art quilts. The narrow binding is less obtrusive and lets the fabric art of the top shine.

Randomly sew together leftover 2¼" strips with 45-degree angle seams for a spiral effect. I love this look, especially with striped fabrics. This can be spectacular, especially on kids' quilts and scrappy quilts.

Tip: Use binding the same color as the border fabric if you want the eye to stay in the borders, especially if there is appliqué present. Use contrasting binding to make the eye bounce back to the body of the quilt, to accent a color or fabric, or if you want to frame the quilt.

Quilting Tips

NEEDLES

Use Sharps needles for cotton and natural fibers. The sharp points easily pierce the natural fibers. Use Ball Point needles for polyester and knits. The rounded point pushes the fibers apart and will not cut them. This reduces raveling of knitted fabrics such as those used to make tee-shirt quilts.

Most quilting machine manufacturers have machined the hook of the bobbin assembly exclusively for their own specified needles. Use the manufacturer's recommended needle for trouble-free quilting. If you try other needles you may hear clicking sounds or worse. They may not give you the best stitch quality, even if you re-time your machine.

Find out which needle sizes you can use without having to re-time your machine. Always keep the distance from the very top of your needle shank to the top of the needle eye the same. If that distance changes, you will need to re-time your machine. (Refer to your machine's manual.) Stay with the same family of needles for best results.

To make sure the needle is straight, roll it on the edge of a table. It will be easy to feel with your fingertips if it is bent.

If your thread is constantly breaking, you may need to move up a needle size. The needle eye needs to be 15%–35% larger than the thread. To test, hold a length of thread in a vertical position with the machine needle threaded onto it. Spin the needle down the thread. If it spins easily, the needle is the correct size. When all else fails, rethread your machine.

Quilting Tips

If you are a beginner and a bit wobbly, keep in mind that titanium needles are harder to break but they will bend if hit and can get caught in your bobbin area. They may damage your hook assembly during removal. Regular polished needles tend to break cleanly and have a better chance of staying out of your bobbin area, which makes them a good choice while learning. Also, choose a larger needle size when learning. Larger needles do not flex as much, so if you keep moving the machine or fabric after the needle stops, they are less likely to break.

As you get more proficient and breaking a needle is a rare occurrence, then titanium needles are a good choice. They last longer than regular needles and can be used to quilt 6–7 quilts. If you are using a regular machine needle, change it with every quilt. If you are using a traditional sit-down machine, change your needle after approximately every 8 hours of quilting.

Tip: Larger needles will accommodate more thread types since the thread stays in the front groove of the needle, allowing the needle and thread to go into the layers of fabric, batting, and backing as one unit. If your thread breaks straight across, it is caused by the thread not being completely in the front groove, so it is cut off at the top of the needle eye. Move up a needle size.

If your thread breaks and the end looks like a curlicue, the thread is stretching as it breaks. Lower the thread tension.

PRESSING

Initial pressing of the quilt top may not be necessary. If there are only surface wrinkles, not sharp creases, they will quilt out without ironing. Lay the quilt top out on a flat surface or drape it over the table/frame, gently spritz with water, and leave it overnight. This is also true for the backing. Before spritzing, be sure there is no embroidery floss or unwashed, heavily-dyed fabrics in the quilt top that can bleed color.

You may need to re-press the sashing seam allowances away from the center, enabling stitching in the ditch without changing thread colors.

QUILT LABELS

Apply labels after machine quilting. Press the edges under and pin baste or thread baste for more accurate placement. Be careful that stitches do not go through the quilt top.

If the quilt label is already sewn on the backing, load the backing so the label is high enough from the bottom edge of the finished quilt after machine quilting and will not be cut off when trimmed back for the binding.

SAMPLER QUILTS

Sampler quilts do not necessarily need a different quilting design for every block. Instead, treat every shape in the entire quilt the same, regardless of which block they appear in. Triangles get one design, squares get another, rectangles a different design, and backgrounds still another. That way you will not have to come up with so many compatible patterns, let alone resize and mark. Sampler quilts are fun again.

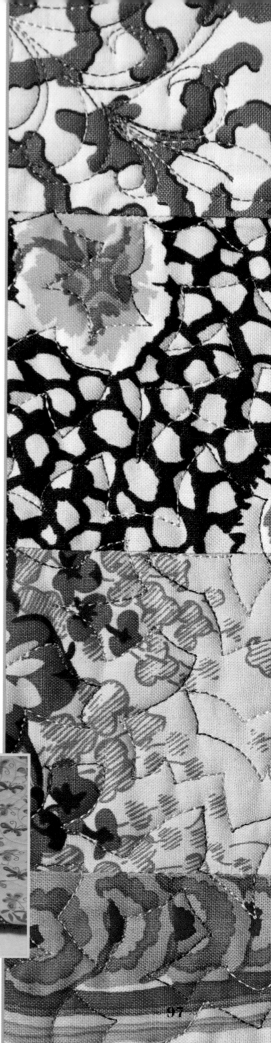

SEAM ALLOWANCES SHADOWING THROUGH

Pull back the dark seam allowance with a long straight quilt pin while the quilt is loaded.

Grade the seams before loading so the lighter fabric completely covers the dark fabric.

Re-press seams to dark fabric before loading.

Baste back seam allowances or pin during quilting.

SECURING THREADS

Secure knots with Fray Check or other seam sealant, especially if you are worried that nylon or polyester thread knots may not hold.

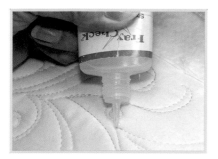

Use a self-threading needle or a long needle with a large eye to bury thread tails. Bury them at least ½" along the stitching line in the opposite direction of the threadpath.

SLEEVE

Construct a hanging sleeve with more fullness on the outer side than the quilt side so a rod or pole will not show when the quilt is hung. The quilt will hang perfectly flat from the top.

Sew the sleeve to the top ⅛" from the raw edge of the trimmed quilt. Then sew the binding ¼" from the raw edge on front of the quilt, catching all the layers.

Baste a ½" inch pleat in the outer fabric so it can be opened for additional fabric for larger diameter poles.

RIGHT: MORNING GARDEN, detail. Made by Ulla Shierhorn, Paducah, KY, and quilted by the author.

Quilting Tips

If you need to temporarily pin on a sleeve, use very large safety pins and space them closely to minimize the stress they put on the fabric.

WASHING YOUR QUILT

If the quilt was marked, the first washing should be two cycles of plain water—both the wash and rinse cycle—with no detergent or soap. Use a hand wash/gentle setting or simply soak for 10 minutes. Gently spin and follow with the rinse cycle. Lay the quilt out in the yard on a clean white sheet and block to dry. This will remove all the chalk and soluble marker. I can almost smell the sunshine.

SQUARE UP CORNERS AFTER QUILTING

When trimming the quilt batting, you want to trim back at the proper dimension for the binding type. Typically you will rotary cut ¼" beyond the raw edge of the quilt top leaving ¼" of batting and backing extending beyond its edge. For self binding, trim the back 2" beyond the quilt top. For fleece and flannel you may want to leave a bit more.

Quilting can distort the corners, especially if they are mitered. To square up the corner, lay a cutting ruler over the corner, squaring up the edges to a 90-degree angle. Trim the batting and backing, lining up the edges at 90 degrees. The quilt top corners will not be squared but the batting and backing will be. As long as the discrepancy between the quilt top and the batting is less than ¼", sewing the binding will catch the edges of the quilt top and you will have true 90-degree angles at the corners.

Cut your binding strips 2¼" wide. Fold in half lengthwise, wrong sides together, and press. Align the raw edges of the binding with the edge of the quilt top and sew with a ¼" seam. Turn to the back and hand finish. Compressing the extra batting in the binding will ensure that the binding is filled with batting and that the binding will measure the same size on the front as on the back—a point many judges will check.

LEFT AND OPPOSITE: MORNING GARDEN, detail. Made by Ulla Shierhorn, Paducah, KY, and quilted by the author.

Specialty Work

When you are quilting for others instead of yourself, it is important that there is a clear understanding on the part of both the quilter and the customer about what is to be done.

TAKING IN THE QUILT TOP FOR PROFESSIONAL QUILTING

Measure the quilt and backing with your customer present. Fix any problem before you start investing your time. Make certain you have enough backing by folding the top and backing in quarters and laying the top directly on the backing, aligning the center corner and folds (see page 11). You will be able to see if the backing fabric extends beyond the quilt top by at least 4".

Complete the check-in form (page 110). The information is as much for you as it is for the customer.

Do not take any thread from the customer. It may be too old or not of high commercial quality for our high-speed, multi-directional machines.

Make the customer aware of batting choices. Do not guarantee any craft batting that would be used in smaller craft projects like stuffing pincushions or the like. It's not designed for use in quilts.

Use the checklist to determine batting selection, thread, backing, thread path density, and so on (see page 110). You do not want to quilt any more than is necessary yet still meet the customer's desires and expectations. Include a discussion about pattern selection and placement. Remember your three sets of coordinating quilting designs and batting sampler (page 93). If a customer has more than three choices, she may become confused and not be able to make a decision.

Be sure to ask, "Is your top pressed and threads clipped to your satisfaction?" Additional charges may be incurred if not.

Specialty Work

THREAD

Audition at least three thread options. You will be amazed how what seems like a bizarre choice can turn out to be the just the right addition. Try to blend colors for an overall look, especially for random square blocks and high contrast fabrics. Avoid using white on scrappy quilts as it ends up looking like string. Use tan or deep warm beige instead.

Stabilize the quilt first, with high contrast thread, stitching the verticals first, then the horizontals. If stabilizing batik fabrics, try to stay near a seam ditch so the holes are not so noticeable when the basting thread is removed.

Choose the lightest color for ditching to match the background. Use a 50-wt or lighter thread for ditching and a heavier thread for more decorative work.

I prefer to quilt the entire top in one color, baste off the bottom and unpin from the leaders, then go back and stitch the other colors. It saves time from changing threads for each advance of the quilt.

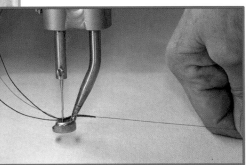

Use an embroidery tie off to change threads. Loop the current thread as if to form a knot, pass the new thread through the loop, and tighten to finish the knot. You can pull the knot through all thread guides and needle eye without rethreading the machine.

Use warm creams to browns in the bobbin for warm variegated threads. Use cool grays in the bobbin for cool variegated threads. Use black in the bobbin for brights and neon variegated threads.

Use "twist" threads (a two-ply thread where both plies are a different color) on hand dyeds and batiks. (My favorite!)

Take up extra thread loops that occasionally appear on the surface by inserting a large heavy pin under the fabric, catching the individual stitch from the side, and pulling the extra thread in the loop into the batting.

Use permanent fabric pens to color a light thread that has mistakenly crossed into a darker fabric area while quilting and to blend in knots on the backing. Also color in construction threads if a seam is separating, exposing the thread.

STITCHING IN THE DITCH

The "ditch" is on the low side of the seam, the side opposite where the seam allowances are pressed.

Always ditch the sashing; it is the skeleton of the quilt. Educate your customers about pressing seam allowances away from the sashing and borders so you can stitch in the ditch without changing thread colors.

Some patterns will overpower the piecing or may never rise to the beauty of the piecing at all. In these cases, it is just best to ditch the blocks and let the true beauty of the piecing shine.

If you don't enjoy in-the-ditch stitching, charge more for it.

EMBELLISHED QUILTS

If the quilt is embellished with ribbon, tape over it so the hopping foot does not get caught under the ribbon. Tape over or remove buttons and other embellishments. Use low tack painter's tape so it does not remove the nap of shiny surfaces on ribbons or fabrics.

Use tape or pins to hold back 3-D flowers, flaps, Prairie Points, etc., around seams.

Specialty Work

Use the one-step trapunto method, inserting an extra piece of batting, cut ⅛" larger than the shape of the appliqué, between the quilt top and quilt batting. As you quilt around the appliqué shape, the extra batting is secured, enabling you to achieve a true trapunto while the quilt is loaded.

Always stitch along the edge of an appliqué shape. Do not echo quilt ¼" away from the shape as that will raise the background fabric, which will visually become part of the appliqué shapes itself. Or you can use a fill-in pattern around the appliqué instead, quilting within that ¼" area to secure the fabric without actually catching the appliqué.

MAJESTIC BLOOMS, 39" x 45", detail, made by Ruth L. Young, Paducah, KY. Quilting and trapunto by the author.
MYSTIC BLOOMS pattern by Sew Be It.

BACKING ART

When the backing is pieced or includes art or a label that must align with the quilt top, special care must be taken to center the top on the backing.

Fold the top and backing in quarters and lay the top on the backing, aligning the folds and center fold corners. Orient the quilt as it will be loaded and measure the extra backing fabric that extends beyond the bottom edges of the quilt top. Subtract 2"–4" from that dimension if it is a large quilt. Subtract 1"–2" if it is a lap quilt or a small wallhanging. The result is the number of inches you should drop down the top edge of the quilt from the edge of the backing. (Do not double the number.)

Orient the top edge of the quilt top that number of inches from the top edge of the backing, keeping in mind the loft of the batting and number of times it rolls around the take-up roller. Thicker batting requires a greater offset.

The batting should extend at least ½" above the top edge of the quilt top to allow for the ¼" trimming for binding, so the binding will be filled and not flat.

LEFT AND OPPOSITE: MY DAINTY BOUQUET QUILT, details. Made by Pat Lewis, Paducah, KY and quilted by David Sweezea, Judy's Stitch in Time Quilt Shop, with digitized Terry Twist pattern.

> **Tip:** If a label is already sewn to the backing, make sure it will be above the bottom edge when positioning the quilt and not cut off when the excess backing fabric is trimmed.

Place a safety pin on the centers of each side of both the quilt top and backing. Place safety pins every 8" from the center pin to the top edge of the quilt. As you advance the quilt, by the time you reach the pins at the center, they should line up, ensuring that you won't run out of backing at the bottom edge of the quilt.

ZIPPERS

Quick and easy to use, zippers let you stitch right on your longarm machine without removing the leaders. You may want to pin and machine baste first. Be sure to clamp both sides of the leaders for even application.

Extra sets of zippers allow you to pin quilts ahead of time and have them ready to load (Resources, page 108). They are great time savers when you have to switch between quilts.

TIMESAVING TIPS

❋ Let a quilt hang on a design wall for a time if you need to come up with a plan. By the time you quilt it, having thought about it for a long time, it will quilt up quickly and may be your best quilt yet.

❋ Mark the quilt top before loading with chalk mechanical pencils, then erase the chalk with an air compressor or Velcro-style clothes brush.

❋ Calculate panto placement and repetitions with the online calculator at **www.quiltscomplete.com.**

Specialty Work

❋ Consider basic design principles as you select your quilting designs.

> **Contrast**—between straight piecing lines and curved quilting lines
>
> **Balance**—even distribution of quilting across the quilt top
>
> **Simplicity**—plain lines without embellishment
>
> **Scale**—the size of the quilting design in relation to the quilt's measurements
>
> **Repetition**—the effect of repeating the same design over and over multiple times

❋ Buy every size of stencils and templates of the one design that you fall in love with; you'll always use them.

❋ If a pattern does not fit evenly in your borders, insert a motif in the center between quilting designs to fit patterns without re-scaling.

❋ Increase the corner block to an L shape to fit border patterns without re-scaling.

❋ Use parallel lines for fills and background quilting; they go with anything.

❋ Use seam lines as center lines and only quilt half of a stencil pattern when the whole design is too big.

❋ Take pictures of corner turns or trace your corner designs onto Glad® Press'n Seal® wrap so you don't have to unroll the quilt to see what you did if you cannot remember when you get to the end.

❋ Use grid paper or The PatternGrid® mat (see Resources, page 108) for design layout and pantograph quilting.

❋ Have 2 or 3 go-to patterns that you can free-motion quilt without marking that will go with any style quilt.

❋ Use calculator tape to divide spaces (page 25).

LEFT AND OPPOSITE: **Quilting samples made by the author.**

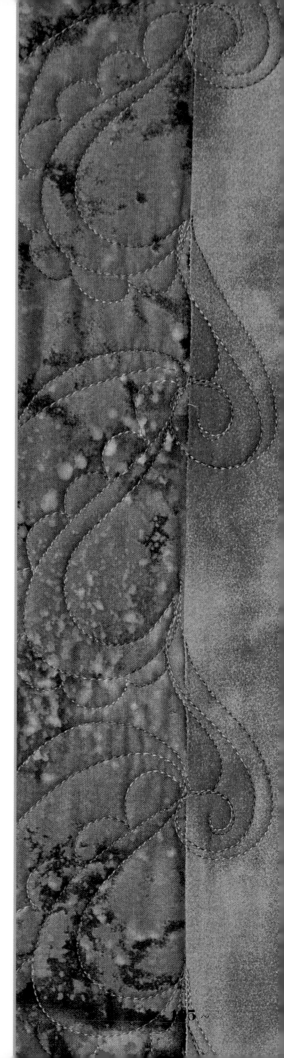

TRIMMING THE QUILT AFTER MACHINE QUILTING

Trim the quilt sandwich leaving ¼" of batting and backing beyond the raw edges so when the raw edges of the binding and quilt top are lined up, there is batting and backing in the turned over binding.

If the backing is turned to the top for a self binding, leave at least 2" beyond the raw quilt top edge, since you need to fold the fabric back to the inside for added stability and a clean edge.

If the quilt top is not square, square up the backing and batting at the corners without cutting the top.

Trim ½" beyond for thicker fabrics like fleeces and Minky.

The binding should be filled with batting and backing and measure the same dimension in from the edge of the front and the back, particularly on quilts that will be judged. You can easily find that out by pinching the sewn binding between your thumb and forefinger to see if they match. Use no fewer than 11 stitches per inch with an embroidery blindstitch to secure the binding on the back.

Trim the quilt back for binding before it leaves your studio. Trimming looks professional and your customer will be ready to do the binding, which will get the quilt out in the world faster with accolades and recommendations for you.

FINALLY . . .

We are all in this together. I hope this book has helped you and given you greater confidence in handling some very pesky problems. Use it as a resource when you are facing new challenges.

And above all enjoy the process!

Yours in the love of quilting,

Sally

Terminology

Advance *(the quilt)*—move the exposed area of the quilt where the machine passes over the fabric after the quilting is completed by turning the rollers

architectural vellum *or "thumbnail" paper*—translucent 4lb–7lb tracing paper available from architectural supply stores used to trace patterns; tears away easily when stitched through

craft foam—thin, 2mm, lightweight sheets of smooth, flexible crafting material that can easily be cut with scissors

baste off—stitch across the bottom edge of a quilt through all three layers so the backing, batting, and top are controlled by the backing roller, allowing the quilt to be rolled back and forth from top to bottom during the quilting process

leader—heavy stretch-resistant cotton duck, canvas, or other fabric that is fastened to the rollers, making it possible to load quilt layers with pins or zippers for the quilting process

medallion quilting pattern—a stand-alone quilting design; a mini-Walking Border

panto/pantograph—a long paper pattern usually traced from the back of the quilting machine by following with a stylus or laser pointer; used to stitch a custom pattern onto the quilt

Shadow Rhythms—closely repeated patterns that have both open, unquilted (negative) areas and heavily stitched (positive) areas that create shadows across the surface of the quilt

LEFT AND OPPOSITE: MOUNTAINS I HAVE CLIMBED, details. Full quilt on page 13.

start and stop designs—small motifs used to begin and end a larger design such as a medallion quilting pattern or Walking Border

stitch in the ditch—stitching along the low side of a seam, that is, the side opposite from where the seam allowances were pressed; especially effective along sashings and borders as it stabilizes the structure of the quilt top

Terry Twist® pattern—gently undulating, asymmetrical design that easily adapts to squares, triangles, and other straight, multi-sided shapes, eliminating the need for stitching in the ditch; can be quickly stitched without marking; perfect for Log Cabin-style blocks, random squares, and more

threadpath—the line of quilting stitches; the spacing should be no larger than the batting manufacturer's recommendation for the maximum distance between quilting lines

timing—the precise machine adjustment where the bottom hook assembly picks up the thread from the low position at the back of the needle and completes the stitch

twist threads—two-ply threads where both plies are a different color

Walking Border—a technique for quilting shapes along a seam or marked spine at a 45-degree angle; the spine itself need not be stitched, but rather is created by the movement of stitching the shapes on either side of it

zippers—long zippers attached to the entire length of the leaders with corresponding material pinned to the backing and quilt top for easy and quick loading

Resources

Architectural Thumbnail Paper
www.draftingsuppliesdew.com
Search "tracing paper"

Bohin Mechanical Chalk Pencil
extra fine 9mm
www.amazon.com

Chalk Cartridge Set
www.clotilde.com

Colorado Quilting Company, LLC
www.coloradoquiltingcompany.com
for The PatternGrid® mat

Columbia River Quilting & Designs
http://columbiariverquilting.com
DBK Stencil Plastic

Flexible Ruler
www.sewforless.com

Quilts Complete
Pantograph Quilting Patterns for Longarm,
Home, Domestic Quilters and Computerized
Quilting Machines
online pantograph placement calculator
http://quiltscomplete.com

The Quilting Connection
Zippers
www.longarmconnection.com

David Sweezea
digitized quilt patterns
Judy's Stitch In Time Quilt Shop
67 South Main
Winchester, KY 40391
859-744-7404
http://judys-stitch-in-time.com

Terry Twist® Patterns
www.sallyterry.com

Wright's EZ® Quilting Tape Go Round™ Highlighter Tape
½" x 3 yards translucent low-tack repositionable
color highlighter tape
www.createforless.com

Hooked On Feathers, by Sally Terry, American Quilter's Society, 2008.

Pathways to Better Quilting: 5 Shapes for Machine Quilt Patterns, by Sally Terry, American Quilter's Society, 2004.

OPPOSITE: MY DAINTY BOUQUET QUILT, detail.
Made by Pat Lewis, Paducah, KY, and quilted by
David Sweezea, Judy's Stitch in Time Quilt Shop,
with digitized Terry Twist pattern.

SAMPLE CHECK-IN FORM

[Quilter's name and contact information]

Order # _____

Name

Address   Apt.

City   State   Zip

Shipping Address

Quilt Description

Work Phone   Home Phone   Cell

Email

Thread Cotton	Poly	Variegated	Metallic Other _____
Top of Quilt	Marked Not Marked	Quilt top up	
Batting	Supplied W & N	80-20 Poly Other	
Backing	Pieced Y N		
	Top Marked Y N	Directional Fabric Y N	
	Used as binding Y N	Seam Direction H V	
	Seam Allowance Press open	Press side	
	Washed Y N	Size _____	
Label and Back Art	Y N Comments_____		
Marking	Do not mark	Chalk	Air/Water Soluble UV pencil
Fabric Prep	Clip threads	Clip points	Iron Wash Prep backing
Binding	Prep binding	Sew Binding F	Sew Binding B
	Purchase binding $_____	Prep backing hr. _____	
Trim Backing	Do not trim ½" ¼" 1"	2" other_____	
Turn Quilt	Y N Fee $_____		
Express Charge	Y N Fee $ _____		
Additional supplies	Y N Fee $ _____		

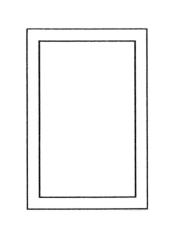

Outer Border   Top L average   _____
Inner Border   Top W average   _____
Additional Borders
Sashings   Backing W   _____
Quilt Body   Backing L   _____
Thread

Notes:

About the Author

Sally Terry's quilting path began at the age of three, sewing doll clothes for her paper dolls. Through her teen years she made all her own clothing and tailored her suits and coats, including bound buttonholes, sewn on Grandma's Featherweight. Sally began professional longarm machine quilting in 1999. With her graphic background and heart of a teacher, she "cannot get her ideas out there fast enough."

Her joyful enthusiasm for sharing results manifests itself in full day workshops for longarm, midarm, and shortarm machine quilters in her Paducah, Kentucky, studio. She is a member of the Instructor Program for Janome-America Sewing Machines. She teaches at major shows and markets nationwide including AQS, MQX, MQS, HMQS, Innovations, Vermont Quilt Festival, Canadian Quilt Show, Quilting on the Waterfront, and Houston.

Her students enjoy her relaxed way of teaching machine quilting that encourages confidence and a joy of learning. Sally approaches the information in her classes from the student's point-of-view with in-depth knowledge that is creative and inspirational.

Sally specializes in running different threads and free-motion quilting with a true touch of creativity. Her concepts have become common practice for beginning machine quilters. She feels that you do not have to copy her exactly to be productive and truly successful without unstitching, and that is a breath of fresh air for all quilters.

A blue-ribbon quilter, Sally's AQS books *Pathways to Better Quilting* (2004) and *Hooked On Feathers* (2008) are both proclaimed classics. Her beginner friendly technique of five basic shapes for machine quilting helps one easily choose and quilt perfect patterns. The popular Terry Twist® series of continuous-line templates, stencils, and patterns are used worldwide.

In addition, she produced three longarm videos: *Care and Adjustment*, *Getting Ready to Quilt*, and *Creative Thread Guide Video*. She has written numerous articles for professional quilting magazines, and has many quilts featured in *American Patchwork & Quilting* and numerous quilting publications and catalogs by Better Homes and Gardens. Sally currently has six published pattern packs and has appeared on *Quilt Central TV* and *American Quilter*.

As an author, pattern designer, lecturer, instructor, and quilter, Sally says, "I feel I was born with an entrepreneurial spirit. Creating several businesses from scratch has given me valuable knowledge of marketing and business strategies that apply directly to professional machine quilters. A lifetime of experiences in marketing, advertising, and sales gives a fresh insight to machine quilters in today's competitive environment."

other AQS Books

This is only a small selection of the books available from the American Quilter's Society. AQS books are known worldwide for timely topics, clear writing, beautiful color photos, and accurate illustrations and patterns. The following books are available from your local bookseller, quilt shop, or public library.

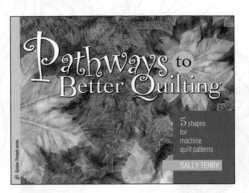

#6509   US $22.95

#8238   US $26.95

#7732   US $24.95

#8234   US $24.95

#6803   US $22.95

#7015   US $22.95

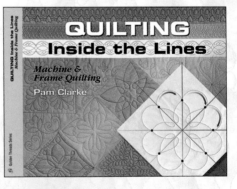

#7072   US $24.95

#6006   US $25.95

#8022   US $24.95

LOOK for these books nationally.
CALL or **VISIT** our website at

1-800-626-5420
www.AmericanQuilter.com